FINDING

FULFILLING WORK

A 21st Century Career Guide for Millennials

by Adele Barlow

FINDING FULFILLING WORK: A 21ST CENTURY
CAREER GUIDE FOR MILLENNIALS

Copyright © 2016 Outbound Books

Copyright © 2016 Adele Barlow

All rights reserved

Published by: Outbound Books™

Cover Design by: Adele Barlow, Catherine Chi & Iván Cruz

www.outbound-books.com

No idea what to do with the rest of your life? This book is where you start.

Careers have become increasingly complex in an era of globalisation and technological advances. Getting a credential and gaining an education have become two separate things. These days, if you want to find work you love, you need to rely on your own exploration instead of waiting for a degree to point you in the right direction.

Finding work you love in the 21st century is about taking a LEAN approach to career development (Learn, Experiment, Achieve and Network). No matter what you are currently doing, this book helps you to take control of your career and steer yourself in a more positive direction.

Using a wide range of stories, it is based on years of experience helping hundreds of smart, driven and lost millennials through the early stages of career change. It is a crucial first step in any recent graduate's journey towards fulfilling work.

TABLE OF CONTENTS

ABOUT THE AUTHOR

Through working with Escape the City, a community of motivated corporate professionals who want to "do something different" with their careers, Adele Barlow found herself quasi-counselling top graduates from the world's leading universities. These bright millennials had followed all the rules, taken "safe" and "sensible" jobs, then found themselves feeling lost.

After accidentally moonlighting as their makeshift therapist and regularly writing for The Huffington Post, Adele trained in cognitive behavioural coaching with the British Psychological Society and started the boutique publishing house Outbound Books, which produces transition psychology books for Generation Y.

In the final year of her undergraduate degree, she co-founded yMedia, an award-winning social enterprise that created digital campaigns for charities. Over the past decade she has also produced digital marketing content and events for various startups, corporations and agencies.

Read more about the author here: www.adelebarlow.com
Read more about the publisher here: www.outbound-books.com
Join Escape the City here: www.escapethecity.org

"I didn't invent the language or the mathematics I use. I make little of my own food, none of my own clothes. Everything I do depends on other members of our species and the shoulders that we stand on. And a lot of us want to contribute something back to our species and to add something to the flow. It's about trying to express something in the only way that most of us know how — because we can't write Bob Dylan songs or Tom Stoppard plays. We try to use the talents we do have to express our deep feelings, to show our appreciations of all the contributions that came before us, and to add something to that flow."

— Steve Jobs

AUTHOR'S NOTE

*"If you can do anything setting out, or along the way—because
it's never too late to start again—figure out who you are.
What do you love to do? How do you want to live? Then,
don't let a career drive you, let passion drive your life.
That may not get you up any ladder, but it will make your
trip down a long and winding road more interesting."*

— *Randy Komisar*

Somewhere around my final semester and college graduation,
I went through a delayed adolescent rebellion, where I started
having arguments with my father over where I should steer my
career. A straight-A student since primary school, I reached a
point at 20 years old that I think most people reach at 13, when
they realise that they *can* do stuff their parents don't want them
to do. Sadly my "rebellion" did not involve popping pills and/or
smashing bottles against the wall but instead involved moving
countries and setting up a startup that connected digital media
students with charities.

Despite my nerdy interpretation of a "conflict" phase, I felt an
acute sense of existential confusion around where the boundaries
between my parents and I ended: what did I "owe" them and
what did I "owe" myself? Was I being selfish and ungrateful if
I followed a path they disagreed with? I partly blame it on my

Eurasian roots: in Asia, family plays a different role than it does in the West. What my Western friends can see as subservient, my Asian friends can see as dutiful.

Being Eurasian, my Western self would tell me to "follow my dreams" while my Asian self would frown, scoff, and tell me to "grow up". Yet didn't growing up mean separating from your parents? Or did it mean separating from your individual desires and taking care of your parents? In my case, growing up meant some heavy debates with my very traditional Dad over what I was going to do once I left university.

Goodbye Career, Hello Success

This is why, during a flight between Wellington and Auckland back in 2008, one of the most dangerous things I could have done for my mind at the time was to read a Harvard Business Review article by Randy Komisar, a well-known Silicon Valley investor. The article was called "*Goodbye Career, Hello Success*" and described Komisar's career story:

"By conventional standards, my résumé is a disaster. Eleven companies in 25 years, not to mention a crazy quilt of jobs: community development manager, music promoter, corporate lawyer, CFO at a technology start-up, and chief executive at a video game company, just to name a few. I zigged, then I zagged, then I zigged some more. By my résumé alone, no one should hire me. Except that these days, plenty of companies would. And they do. At last, my "non-career" career makes perfect sense — to them and to me."

Komisar went to Harvard Law School, acted as senior counsel for Apple Computer, served as CEO for LucasArts Entertainment and Crystal Dynamics and as a "virtual CEO" for such companies as WebTV and GlobalGiving. He is a founding director of TiVo. He now works at investment firm Kleiner Perkins Caufield & Byers and lectures on entrepreneurship at Stanford University.

At the time of reading Komisar's article, I was running a startup in New Zealand, having just graduated from university. It was called yMedia. We were supported by a philanthropic foundation and corporate sponsors like Microsoft, IBM, and Saatchi & Saatchi. While on the surface, we were winning awards and appearing in national press, whenever I spoke to my parents, I was racked with guilt over having found something I loved this much this soon. Shouldn't I have had to pay my dues in some corporate graduate scheme first?

We had won seed funding while I was in my final year of university, so I had gone straight from the classroom into this incredible adventure. I was 21 at the time (professionally, a foetus at that point) so I can see why I was unsure about my capabilities.

Somewhere between getting disillusioned by national government bureaucracy and realising that reliance on sponsorships and grants was not a sustainable revenue model, my business partner and best friend Pam and I decided to hand the reigns over to successors, who grew yMedia and transformed their own partnership into what remains a successful creative agency. Pam headed to Canada and I headed to London, for law school, which ended up teaching me what James Joyce meant when he declared "mistakes are the portals of discovery".

ESCAPE THE CITY

Sitting at home on Facebook, I saw a family friend post a link from a website called Escape the City. I had just moved to the

UK a month or two earlier and had dropped out of law school soon after my first class. I was doing an internship with a digital media investment firm, but on the whole, I was feeling listless. Though I couldn't see it at the time, I was waiting to be rescued.

I wanted a prescription for what to do with this next phase of life. My university had not given me answers, neither had yMedia, neither had law school; so I was looking to my parents, friends, peers, my boyfriend at the time, trying to find clues to a puzzle that I felt like everyone else had already figured out.

I wanted a career where I got to write and create and build businesses that I believed in. I wanted to throw myself behind causes that mattered. I had felt so *alive* with yMedia; so excited, curious, passionate, laser-focused. I wanted *that* but with a grown-up pay cheque. Then again, when I was younger, I had also wanted Santa Claus to exist.

When I stumbled upon Escape the City, it resonated with me on a deep level, because it reminded me that while I couldn't control certain things, I could control my choices. A few weeks after discovering that Facebook link, I found myself knocking at the door of co-founder Rob Symington's house, and stayed in touch with both him and his co-founder Dom Jackman over the years as we became friends. Years later, and after they'd raised funding, I officially came on board to help them grow the business as one of their first employees.

The more I learned about 21st century career development through being involved with Escape the City, the more I became comfortable with my own choices. I wrote a couple of books on career change, one about MBAs and one about leaving the legal profession, and through my own experiences, I learned that the path to finding fulfilling work is not always clear-cut.

I thought I had been struggling with finding fulfilling work, but what I had actually been struggling with was knowing what to commit to. I had been scared of committing to something that would later turn out to be a waste of time, because in many ways, the yMedia dream had not panned out the way I had originally envisioned and that had been so painful to accept.

I also knew that if I failed to commit to anything, I would never develop depth of expertise, and that was something I craved. So while I was working with Escape the City, I made sure to keep doing the things that I had seen work for me in the past: I treated each workday as a learning opportunity, I made sure to keep experimenting with the things I was interested in, I set myself goals that increased my confidence in the areas I wanted to improve in, and I kept making an effort to meet new and interesting people.

These principles around making an effort to Learn, Experiment, Achieve and Network are the principles that formed the foundation of the LEAN framework that I introduce and discuss in this book. They have been reinforced by my experiences in training as a cognitive behavioural coach with the British Psychological Society.

THE LEAN GRADUATE

In short, the LEAN framework is based on the idea that undergraduate degrees these days tend to be more of a social signal to prospective employers as opposed to practical tools for knowing how to enter and navigate today's workforce.

While this book is aimed at recent graduates who are struggling to figure out where to go when they leave university, I believe LEAN principles of career development are just as relevant to those at a later stage in their career.

These days, I am the marketing manager at a legal tech startup called Lexoo, which helps businesses to find a lawyer. I write for The Huffington Post and I publish books on Amazon through a company I started called Outbound Books. Now and then, I still help out at Escape the City.

While I might not have all the answers, I learned loads of interesting concepts and stories through Escape the City and through training as a coach, which brought me some much-needed clarity and peace. I wanted to share them here, to help friends and strangers going through the inevitable existential crisis that seems to haunt so many ambitious and socially conscious young professionals.

The Escape the City ethos has always been to start small, to worry less about "finding your passion" and to instead pay more attention to figuring out your interests and what excites you. Escape started as a blog and newsletter – literally in a basement – and now reaches over 250,000 members around the world.

When I enter Escape the City HQ in London today, I get the same feeling as whenever I walk through the doorway of my parents' home. It is familiar and warm and has taught me so much. These learnings are what I wanted to pass on to anyone who currently feels the way I felt when I dropped out of law school: like I was stupid for not knowing what my "passion" was. Like I was a failure because I had put so much pressure on myself to "achieve" throughout school and now felt like I wasn't living up to my full potential, whatever the hell that was. Like I was flaky, or lazy, or all these things that weren't true – they were just silly stories I was telling myself.

Finding fulfilling work is about finding a sense of belonging in the wider world. It's about learning where you feel like you belong to something larger than yourself. When I had no idea what to do with my career, the days were long and the world was boring. The more engaged I became in my work, the more time ran faster than I could keep up with it, endless possibilities cracked open, life picked up momentum, I met really interesting people and had fascinating conversations. Ultimately, I felt like a more complete version of myself.

My CV talks about meeting Prime Minister David Cameron at 10 Downing Street and the General-Secretary Ban Ki-moon at the United Nations HQ in Manhattan, but looking back, the real career highlights have been more meaningful and invisible moments, like the first day we ran the Startup MBA at Escape the City, team lunches, and hanging with great colleagues who became great friends.

I did not find my way by listening to my parents or following what I was taught in school. In fact, doing the opposite is what made all the difference. I hope this book can do for graduates what Escape the City did for me: it gave me hope and taught me to have a little more faith in myself. When I was lost, it helped me to see that only I could access my own solutions.

As Randy Komisar wrote: "If you can do anything setting out, or along the way—because it's never too late to start again—figure out who you are. What do you love to do? How do you want to live? Then, don't let a career drive you, let passion drive your life. That may not get you up any ladder, but it will make your trip down a long and winding road more interesting. And in the end, if it makes you feel better, go ahead and call it a career. It doesn't matter. A career is what you make it."

This is all very well in theory, but in practice, it can be hard knowing exactly where to begin. This is why I wrote this book, which I hope helps graduates understand where to proceed next in their journey towards meaningful work. It is based on the real advice that I gave four graduates (whose names I have changed) – Charlie, Nadia, Sam, and Andy, who we meet in the next chapter.

[1]

THE LOST GRADUATES

"The people who have been living in a world which always told them what to do – which made life easy for them and told them what the next step was, and put them on an escalator so to speak – this world never let them discover their weaknesses and failures, not to mention their strengths."

— *Abraham Maslow*

As morning broke in New York, Charlie woke up and shook off the night before. His eyes focused to the light and his mind realised that yet again, he had nowhere in particular to be. This was meant to be liberating, but instead, it felt heavy. For the thousandth time in what seemed like months – although it had really only been a few weeks since his post-graduation travels to Peru – he wished that he didn't feel like such a loser. He heard his parents leave for work and while they didn't mean to insult him by slamming the door, each sound was just a reminder that they, unlike him, had a workplace to show up to every morning.

Over the other side of the Atlantic Ocean, Nadia found herself squished in a lunchtime queue at a busy Starbucks in central London. Her "boss" wanted a skinny soy caramel macchiato, no whipped cream, and a skinny blueberry muffin. She had taken on an unpaid internship at a well-known glossy magazine and she knew she should be thrilled. She was. Yet she often wished that she had the luxury of not having to take on stints like this, pseudo-work for pseudo-bosses who were only a year or two older than her, and really didn't seem to be teaching her much except more about who she didn't want to be.

Across the world in Asia, Sam was trying to keep her eyes open in the middle of a meeting, up near the top of a skyscraper in Kuala Lumpur. She had been up most of the night putting the finishing touches on the Powerpoint presentation that her colleague was leading the people in the room through. Sam had stumbled into this role by accident. Management consulting paid well and she was slowly getting used to the business class flights and the plush hotels that she never even really got to spend time in anyway. Yet she longed for a more creative role, maybe in film or in magazines. Or maybe something more meaningful, like working for a charity.

In Fiji, Andy was splashing around in the ocean with a few children from the village. He loved this life, building a school with a charity on this remote island that could not feel further away from the large city he had grown up in. Still, he knew that it couldn't last forever. He was having so much fun that it often felt too good to be true, and in certain moments, usually right before he fell asleep, he would remind himself to enjoy this while it lasted, because real life was waiting for him back in England. His mind often avoided the question of what he would do next, because it was one that he had absolutely no idea how to answer.

They had worked hard at school. They had gone to good universities. They had graduated with little to no idea of what came next. They were hungry to make something of themselves yet when they grabbed the opportunities that life handed them, something felt like it was missing.

They thought they were searching for something different to do but what they were actually craving was somebody different to be. They were scattered all over the globe and they had never met one another, but their 3am panic attacks were all laced with the same ingredients of chronic anxiety, borderline depression, and a sense that all the hard work had been for nothing.

While I met them all at different times, I felt an immediate sense of connection to each of them, because they helped me to remember the injustice I had felt once leaving university.

* * *

It had taken me a while to realise that the degree I had worked so hard for was actually going to do very little by way of navigating me once I had graduated. My parents and teachers had always led me to believe that as long as I worked hard and got good grades, everything would be okay.

It wasn't like I was homeless, or suffering any real kind of danger or hardship. But upon graduation, I felt confused as to what all that time and effort and money had been spent on. Had I just been jumping through a ton of hoops for no apparent reason?

After the first few hundred conversations I had about this topic with various Escape the City members, I started to notice that I had not been alone in my thinking. So many of us had expected our universities to steer us in some way or another towards the next phase of life and had ended up feeling short-changed by these institutions.

* * *

Few, I think, felt this as acutely as Charlie.

The Educational Ponzi Scheme

"College is nothing more than a baby-sitting service. These students are totally unprepared for the real world."

— *Kelly Cutrone*

Was he hungover?

This was one of those mornings where Charlie couldn't tell.

I'm not, he realised, as his eyes opened. Then he propped himself up on his elbows in bed and as his brain started pulsing to the Macarena in his skull, he realised he could be wrong.

The past few weeks had been a haze of mornings like this and nights like the one before. The main feeling that permeated each day was guilt and worthlessness. His parents were being ridiculously nice about everything and he was grateful for it, but sometimes he wished they were a little harder on him.

"What did you get up to today?" His mother would ask sweetly, and sometimes he wanted to snap at her, but then he would catch himself and force himself to reply calmly.

"Just applied for stuff online."

To jobs that I don't want, which I highly doubt I'll get, he wanted to say.

Sometimes he looked around and wondered – was this what they had been working so hard for? Was this what he was meant to be doing? Sitting at home, applying to companies online who never even replied to him?

Maybe this was a quarter-life crisis, he mused.

* * *

When I met Charlie, I told him that back in as early as 2001, Abby Wilner and Alexandra Robbins wrote an article called, *"QuarterLife crisis, the Unique Challenges of Life in your Twenties."* It argued that a young person struggles greatly in the transition from education to working life – that the real world is harsher than they could have predicted; that life costs more than they expected; and that instead of having frequent performance feedback and visible milestones they are, for the first time, suddenly in charge of their own fates – and they realise, that they have no idea what they want.

The term caught on, and at least every year since, some major publication in some part of the world hooked onto this sociological trend – the Boston Globe ran *"The QuarterLife Crisis"* in 2004; TIME ran the *"Grow Up? Not so fast"* piece in 2005; *"The Odyssey Generation just won't grow up"* appeared in the Sunday Times in 2007; and in August 2010, the New York Times asked: *"What is it about 20somethings?"*

TIME's 2005 piece wrote, "Parents were baffled when their expensively educated, otherwise well-adjusted 23-year-old children wound up sobbing in their old bedrooms, paralyzed by indecision."

What frustrated me about this was that this "quarter-life crisis" term seemed like a huge over-simplification of a pretty significant trend. The label made any upset millennial seem like an over-thinking navel-gazer, when actually, what millennials are facing is a world in which their parents and teachers cannot guide them, because the world has so drastically changed in recent decades.

Before the level of mobility that we experience now, identity was inherited as opposed to constructed. Nowadays, we are free to write our own lives, but with that freedom we also have the potential to get it wrong.

In this era of extended adolescence, we are dealing with what sociologist Zygmont Bauman called "liquid modernity." The existential angst overshadowing the millennial subconscious means that we can find ourselves torn between freedom and security. Creating a liveable balance between the two – embracing responsibility without feeling suffocated by commitments – is a new challenge.

In increasingly globalised, mobile, digital circumstances, this new liquidity means that our mash-up life stories can be arranged and dissembled in whatever city we choose – the paths are no longer as straightforward or as clear, because they are no longer inherited. The idea that we construct our identities, rather than inheriting them, strikes at the root of this new existential anxiety.

The trouble, I explained to Charlie, is when we rely on traditional educational institutions to navigate us out of this quandary, when in fact, the new worthlessness of certain degrees is half the issue. We need to treat *getting a credential* and *getting an education* as separate tasks. These days, an undergraduate degree (especially an Arts degree) tends to be more of a social signal rather than a prescription of what to do with the rest of your life. It can be like a passport as opposed to a boarding pass: we need it in order to leave the country, but we have to make up our own mind about where it is that we want to go.

Charlie had reached a point where he felt completely stagnant. When you leave university, and you're trying to find a job, but nobody will employ you because you don't have any work experience, you start to feel like perhaps there's little point in even trying. I understood what he was going through – it was easy to feel like a victim of what I liked to call the Educational

Ponzi Scheme. However, painting ourselves as victims was not going to help anybody.

I told Charlie that it might help if he educated himself on the broader context of academic inflation.

Academic inflation refers to the idea that if everyone has a bachelor's degree, that means to stand out from the crowd, you need a master's degree. But as soon as everyone gets a master's degree too, you then need a PhD to stand out.

One of the best books I read on the changing function of higher education was *The Global Auction,* written by professors at universities in the United Kingdom. They argue that the idea of "more education is better" has been a widely accepted belief of developed economies. It seems to be a universal belief that college diplomas bestow upon Americans and Europeans a competitive advantage in the global knowledge wars.

However, they challenge such views about how the global economy really works. They break apart conventional wisdom that encourages higher education as the path for the lower class to become middle class and the middle class to become prosperous. Instead, they explore how, as world economies have become more integrated and networked, the market value of American workers is no longer compared to local citizens, but rather is part of a global auction for jobs.

They argue that economists who compare America, Britain, and Germany as head nations (brains) and China and India as body nations (brawn) have overlooked that the new global economy has allowed emerging economies to create a high-skill, low-wage workforce more than able to compete for hi-tech, high-value employment in the head nations.

Historically, college-educated Americans were protected from price competition as long as educated talent was either in limited supply or only available from equally expensive countries like Britain, Germany, and Japan. Now, the authors argue, there is a price competition for expertise. There has been a doubling of the supply of college educated workers in affluent and emerging countries over the past decade, plus companies have invested in technologies to increasingly standardise certain jobs.

There is now an "opportunity trap" which happens when everyone works toward the same strategy such as earning a bachelor's degree or working longer hours to impress the boss. However, the authors argue that most people will view education as a defensive expenditure, necessary to have any chance at improving the middle class standard of living.

Reading *The Global Auction* solidified some suspicions I'd had about a credential being a social signal more than anything else. It was part of a larger debate I had been watching play out, and one of the most interesting leaders in the debate was Peter Thiel, an entrepreneur and billionaire investor who argued that education was one of the last remaining bubbles in America. Students pay a ton of money to attend school, fall into a debt that cannot be erased, and leave school with little to show except a piece of paper.

Arguing that real-world work experience outweighed going to class, Thiel offered to grant a hundred thousand dollars each to a high-potential group of students who drop out of college. Known as the Thiel Felowship, it was an example of an investor putting their money where their mouth was in terms of reshaping how education was delivered. I found his opinions on the education bubble fascinating.

"A true bubble is when something is overvalued and intensely believed," he said. "Education may be the only thing people still believe in in the United States. To question education is really dangerous. It is the absolute taboo."

He argues that like the housing bubble, the education bubble is about security and insurance against the future. Like the housing bubble, excesses are excused by a core collective belief that no matter what happens, this is a solid investment. There is a strong desire to believe that you will always make more money if you are college educated. While based in truth, the bubble gets pushed to unhealthy levels when people kid themselves into thinking that with this investment they are "set" for life.

Whether you called it a bubble or the Educational Ponzi Scheme or plain old academic inflation just getting worse, it clearly sucked not only for the graduates who had invested so much in their institutions but also the parents who often had to host them post-university, at a time when these graduates were meant to be out there making it on their own in the world. Charlie could see that while his parents thought the answer lay in applying to companies online, it was not necessarily going to be that simple.

THE RISE OF UNPAID INTERNSHIPS

"The rich get richer or stay rich, in other words, thanks in part to prized internships, while the poor get poorer because they're barred from the world of white-collar work, where high salaries are increasingly concentrated."

— *Ross Perlin*

The heart of what Charlie was struggling with was that he knew he had to do some kind of internship, but it was most likely going to be unpaid, and he had no idea how to broach this with his parents. As he talked about what he was experiencing, I told him about the concept of shame.

"What personally frustrates me with the Educational Ponzi Scheme is the shame that it provokes in those who leave university not knowing what to do next (which I would argue is most people who do generalist degrees)," I explained. "Shame is a feeling of *being* wrong, and can be differentiated from guilt, which is the feeling of *having done* wrong." Shame is the root cause of so much depression.

I found it unfair that while credentials have become more expensive and arguably more necessary as a social signal, they remain largely futile in terms of career guidance. I saw that increasing armies of graduates started to feel like because their degrees had turned out to be kind of worthless, *they* then felt kind of worthless too.

It seems fair for a slight gap to exist between where education leaves off and employment begins. However, it seems unfair that the gap stretches so broad that a graduate has to then work (unpaid) in order to compensate for the gaps of the degree that they have spent thousands to earn.

What this injustice fosters is an environment that Ross Perlin examines in *Intern Nation*. Perlin argues that internships have exploded in numbers as they have basically become a requirement to gain entry to the labor market, though Perlin views them as "a form of mass exploitation hidden in plain sight". He claims that a large share of interns are unethical if not illegal.

He talks about the resumé "arms race" where an internship becomes less of a learning experience and instead yet another social signal to future employes. He argues that not only do unpaid internships devalue work, but they have also become a site of reproduction of privilege:

"Many internships, especially the small but influential sliver of unpaid and glamorous ones, are the preserve of the upper-middle class and the super rich. These internships provide the already privileged with a significant head start that pays professional and financial dividends over time, as boosters never tire of repeating."

While I completely agree with Perlin's observations, I would add that there does not need to be such a strict level of determinism when it comes to class mobility. While an internship can provide a significant head start, I believe that most successful people reach where they are because of a series of opportunities, and I wonder if there is an over-emphasis or exaggeration on the internship as a magic-bullet solution.

An internship can lead to a valuable mentor but there are other ways to gain access to what an internship can provide. However, Perlin makes some strong points about the role of class in these debates, such as the following:

"For the well-to-do and wealthy families seeking to guarantee their offspring's future prosperity, internships are a powerful investment vehicle, and an instrument of self-preservation in the same category as private tutoring, exclusive schools, and trust funds. Meanwhile, a vast group of low – and middle-income families stretch their finances thin to afford thankless unpaid positions, which are less and less likely to lead to real work, and a forgotten majority can't afford to play the game at all."

Charlie's shame came from the fact that he was from a well-off family who could afford to have him lounge around home while he perused online jobs boards. He had gone to a good school, a good university, and now, when he was meant to be a good young man going off to his good new job, he had nothing to show his parents for the investment they had made in him. This is what was making him feel particularly useless as a human being. Was he being too fussy? Should he really be searching for a job he *loved* or should he just accept whatever came along?

When I talked to Charlie about the issue, I told him about an article by Miya Tokumitsu, discussing how the "do what you love (DWYL)" mantra hides the fact that being able to choose a career primarily for personal reward is a privilege, a sign of socioeconomic class. Thus DWL becomes "a secret handshake of the privileged and a worldview that disguises its elitism as noble self-betterment." Since this was the very name of a workshop series that I had designed at Escape the City, and a strong element of Escape the City's ethos in general, I felt particularly interested in the points the article raised, specifically:

"While DWYL seems harmless and precious, it is self-focused to the point of narcissism. One consequence of this isolation is the division that DWYL creates among workers, largely along class lines. Work becomes divided into two opposing classes: that which is lovable (creative, intellectual, socially prestigious) and that which is not (repetitive, unintellectual, undistinguished). Those in the lovable-work camp are vastly more privileged in terms of wealth, social status, education, society's racial biases, and political clout, while comprising a small minority of the workforce."

I told Charlie how reading that article had made me feel like I should apologise, though what the author was describing wasn't my fault. I was lucky enough to be able to search for work I loved. Did that make me "self-focused to the point of narcissistic", as Tokumitsu put it?

The conclusion that Charlie and I settled on was that everyone is born with certain advantages and disadvantages. Privilege has always existed and shall always continuc to exist. There will always be someone more privileged than you and there will always be someone less so too. The best we can do, surely, is to make the most of whatever privileges we have been given to improve the experiences of others.

After all, while I fell into the "loveable-work camp" of "privileged people" that Tokumitsu describes, a point that resonated with me from Tokumitsu's assessment was the observation that the industries most heavily reliant on interns (fashion, media, and the arts) happen to be feminised. As Tokumitsu says, "Women are supposed to do work because they are natural nurturers and are eager to please; after all, they've been doing uncompensated child care, elder care, and housework since time immemorial."

So I might have a socioeconomic advantage on the one hand, but apparently, a gender disadvantage on the other. Do I choose to focus on all the advantages I've been lucky enough to have been given, or on what some might call a disadvantage? Which approach, I asked Charlie, do you think would empower me more in the long run?

After all, I told Charlie, privilege comes with its own set of questions. It wasn't like the high-flying corporate workers who seemed to be at the golden end of the spectrum had it all figured out. As I had seen from Escape the City and meeting members like Sam, while having a secure salary might symbolise a certain level of freedom, a prestigious job title was also the source of its own set of issues.

A Gold-Starred Sleepwalk

"Some of the most talented individuals in the world
find themselves stuck in an unending holding pattern,
a professional gray zone housing those who have the
most options of all and have failed to convert any of
them for fear of missing out on all the others."

— *Daniel Gulati*

Sam was a management consultant based in New York but stationed in Kuala Lumpur on a three-month project. One morning, she looked in the mirror and felt like she had aged eight years in the past six months. She had been ecstatic when she'd landed a job with her current company.

She loved the way it felt to hand over her business card. While she complained about them on the surface, secretly she loved these all-nighters, the rush of getting something ready by a seemingly impossible deadline.

She hated feeling like her life revolved around work. She hated how little she got to see her friends. She loved the hotels but she hated the constant travel. She loved the pay cheque but she hated what it cost her.

If there was some kind of major event then perhaps she would've had to reconsider, because she knew that this wasn't a way to live a life. This wasn't the way that she wanted to live forever. She'd had interests, once upon a time. She'd created things, joined groups, she'd had friends she would spend entire weekends with. Now it seemed too indulgent to have that much of a social life. Any spare time she did have these days, she spent on the treadmill or on FaceTime with her boyfriend back in New York.

Was it worth it? She never had the time or energy or interest to truly ask herself that question. She'd been so caught up in her head that sometimes she felt the distinct lack of energy emanating from her heart, like it had been told to shut up, and had been so scarred by the experience that it retreated into a silent exile.

It hit her sometimes, right before a meeting began, when she was sitting in a conference room by herself. Alone with her thoughts, in the pause after she realised that there was nothing left to prepare before the others stepped into the room, life would seem eerily still.

For a few calm, terrifying moments, she'd hover above herself and see that she had become a glorified secretary for the balance sheets of massive companies who would never register her existence. She and her colleagues were all just cogs in a meaningless machine, pretending they were important, talking about projections, making arguments and analyses, detailing hypothetical situations so much and so often that sometimes she felt like she herself was becoming a hypothetical person.

* * *

When I met Sam, the first book I pointed her towards was *Excellent Sheep: The Miseducation of the American Elite and the Way to a Meaningful Life*, by former Yale professor William Deresiewicz. When she described that she had been feeling like a ghost version of her former self, I told her about how Deresiewicz described today's Ivy League as a highly competent zombie factory:

"The system manufactures students who are smart and talented and driven, yes, but also anxious, timid, and lost, with little intellectual curiosity and stunted sense of purpose: trapped in a bubble of privilege, heading meekly in the same direction, great at what they're doing but with no idea why they're doing it."

These days, Deresiewicz says, most smart and energetic young people have the opportunity to live a life of meaning and purpose and still make a decent living. As he explains, "This is a very rare opportunity in human history, and the only thing that can screw it up for you is if you allow yourself to buy into the kind of standards that the system works so hard to instil, that desperate need for the constant affirmation of credentials and gold stars, whether in the form of A's or of ultra-high salaries and prestigious titles."

He talks about how American society is so wealthy that most of its young people can live comfortably as a teacher or civil rights lawyer or artist. Though a person may be confined to an ordinary house instead of a Manhattan penthouse or L.A. mansion and drive a Honda instead of a BMW, he asks, "What are such losses when set against the opportunity to do work you believe in, work you're suited for, work you love, every day of your life?"

In an essay preceding his book, *The Disadvantages of an Elite Education,* he talks about how Ivy League high-achievers chastise themselves with guilt over "squandering the opportunities" their parents worked hard to provide. He describes how those who might dream of becoming schoolteachers trip up on the following internal monologue: "What will my friends think? How will I face my classmates at our 20th reunion, when they're all rich lawyers or important people in New York? And the question that lies behind all these: 'Isn't it beneath me?' So a whole universe of possibility closes, and you miss your true calling."

Sam told me that she could completely relate to what Deresiewicz described and that in many ways, although she was getting paid a lot of money, she was starting to wonder what her salary was costing her.

"This isn't what I want to do for the next twenty years," she confessed. "I'm just not sure where I'd even start if I left this though."

While I could have said to Sam that she, like Charlie, was simply feeling the after-effects of the Educational Ponzi Scheme, I wasn't sure how much that would help her. I wanted to point out that if she were to change career paths, she might in fact have to do an unpaid internship or two, which would be a sharp difference from the salary bracket she was on at the moment. I knew that the notion of "excellent sheep" had helped her to understand that she was not alone but I also felt like part of her *liked* being one of the excellent sheep. She might be unhappy but at least she was safe.

So how do we know where to start, when we're sure we don't want to be doing what we're currently doing, but we have no idea what to do if not this? This was the central question that Escape the City was set up to help people answer. Through exploring it over the years, I came up with the LEAN framework, which we explore in the following chapter.

[2]

THE LEAN FRAMEWORK

"Making decisions too early, trying to plan life too carefully, can close doors rather than keep them open. Any time you make a plan, you do it with imperfect information; the further in advance you make that plan, the less information you have. You never know how you will feel or what choices you might face. Take life one step at a time and don't make decisions before you have to."

— *Sheryl Sandberg*

The LEAN framework came about after thousands of hours spent at Escape the City, with a team whose mission it is to help people find work they love. While I was there, I observed how the challenge to find fulfilling work in the 21st century is a new dilemma.

Life is an exchange of information and experiences: we are many things (friends, lovers, citizens, etc.) but we are also cogs in an economic machine, designed to exchange our resources (time and energy) for resources from others (salary and income). We develop skills and knowledge (our "value" to trade) through how the world "uses" us.

Education is meant to catalyse this process, so that when we leave our parents' nest, we can provide resources for our own children. Therefore, we pay for school to optimise our viability as products in the marketplace.

All the content I consumed through my formal education treated knowledge as if it were laid out on a map. It was treated as if knowledge-gathering were a linear experience where we learned the basics in primary school, more advanced notions in secondary school, and at university, we built upon those ideas even further. You weren't allowed to study seventh-form textbooks in third-form classes.

However, upon leaving university, it became clearer to me that so many of the knowledge "maps" of the world no longer existed because the world has become much more complicated. Thanks to the rise of tools like Facebook, there are now entire careers that simply did not exist a decade or two ago, and may not exist in the decades to come. For instance, you can now decide to become a digital marketing specialist who only handles Google advertising, or a teacher who delivers lessons exclusively online. There are new paths being created by technology all the time but there is no telling how long they will last.

This means that we have take more responsibility than ever before for the individual construction of our careers. This is terrifying and liberating at the same time.

Before explaining the LEAN framework, I wanted to introduce a brilliant essay by Escape co-founder Rob Symington called "What Unites People Who Do Work They Love?" I have printed this essay in its entirety below as it provides a foundation for the concepts at the heart of the LEAN framework.

While I was at Escape the City, I worked closely with Rob and absorbed the below through not only spending countless hours with him but also through making similar observations myself.

Seth Godin, who Rob and I both read voraciously over the years, made the following observation, which sums up the seed of the LEAN framework:

"Technology keeps changing the routes we take to get our projects from here to there. It doesn't pay to memorize the route, because it's going to change soon. The compass, on the other hand, is more important than ever. If you don't know which direction you're going, how will you know when you're off course? And yet we spend most of our time learning (or teaching) the map, yesterday's map, while we're anxious and afraid to spend any time at all calibrating our compass."

Similarly, I believe the below essay highlights the foundation on which I based the LEAN principles.

What Unites People Who Do Work They Love? (Rob Symington, Escape the City co-founder)

"I have spent the last 5 years obsessing about what it takes for ambitious and passionate professionals to step off the mainstream career travelator and build a career on their own terms. Through building Escape the City into a global community of 250,000 people and through launching The Escape School in central London I have had the privilege of speaking to countless people about what they want to do with their lives and what is stopping them. Unsurprisingly, most people are really clear on what they don't like about their careers but haven't got a clue when it comes to identifying what it is they'd like to do instead.

The questions for so many of us then are these:

What are we actually aiming at?

What would it feel like to do work we loved?

What should we do to reach a place of deep satisfaction when it comes to work and our careers?

Like with so many things in life, we need role models. When I look at people who do love their work, I see a few unifying characteristics.

1. They pursue and attain excellence.
People I admire who love their work are excellent at some aspect of it. Excellence often leads to autonomy because the better you are at something, the more likely you are to be able to do it on your own terms, to command higher fees, and to have greater control over who you work with and what you work on. Think of any impressive TED speaker – their particular and unique excellence is what has brought them to that stage and it is probably one of the main factors in allowing them to do work they love too. There are no shortcuts. You want a life on your own terms? You're going to have to get damn good at something.

2. They have a clear niche.
There are many roles for generalists throughout the economy (and indeed, portrayed the right way, being a generalist could be a niche in itself). However, people who excel at something often seem to have narrowed things down for themselves. This could be in terms of industry or location or customer segment or service. We live in a complicated, chaotic world and trying to make everyone happy is a sure-fire way of making no one happy. We find this again and again with Escape the City – when we are brave and exclude new opportunities or new customer segments we find we are able to double down on delighting people around a smaller subset of things we consider are really worth pursuing.

3. They are patient.

Building something awesome takes time – be it a skill, a career or a business. Some people come to The Escape School with the expectation that there is some magic formula to work fulfilment, financial security, and happy-ever-after voila. The reality is that every single person whose life you envy or whose career you admire has got to where they are through persistence (and a good dose of luck and chance no doubt).

Check out Maria Popova (the founder of the incredible brainpickings.org). She has been writing for seven years. Like Escape the City, her idea started as a simple blog and a newsletter sent to some friends. Go check out her "About" page to see where patience (as well as excellence and a clear niche) has taken her.

People often say to me, "it's not that I'm scared of putting in the 10,000 hours to become excellent at something, it's that I don't know what my Thing is and I don't want to pick the wrong thing." This is a really elegant trap. The only way we know what we want to do with our lives (or even with the next three years) is by getting out there and trying things. If we never start because we are labouring under the belief that one day we will "Just Know" what it is we want to do with our lives.

4. They make active choices.

If you have read The Escape Manifesto you will have heard us talk about "The Accidentals" – those of us who wake up one day and realise that whatever career path we are on wasn't really of our choosing. People who succeed (in any walk of life – be it investment banking or building schools in Africa) make active choices. They bravely and deliberately exclude options in order to actively choose ones to proceed with. They have their eyes open and know why they are doing what they are doing and what they are getting out of a given situation. There are certainly such things as good choices and bad choices, but believing that there is simply One Choice that we have to take is a trap. If we delay starting until we have found the Right Thing, we'll never start. You don't have to quit your job or take big risks, just pick up a rope anywhere and see where it leads.

5. They have a network of strong allies.

People who succeed have allies. Especially if they are on paths less travelled. The more what you are doing is unconventional, the more you will benefit from having a community around you of likeminded people on similar journeys. Speak to any entrepreneur, freelancer or independent worker and you will find that they have a network of trusted people who they use for support and inspiration. No man / woman is an island. Find your tribe.

6. They enjoy the process.

You are unlikely to have the patience (#3) to become excellent (#1) if you don't enjoy what you do. I have stayed with Escape the City for years for many different reasons, but one of the main ones has been how damn fun it is. Getting good at something that is hard is fun. Building a business with your friends is fun. Calling the shots in your own life is fun. Either way, if it ain't fun for you, you're unlikely to last the course. And, if you are going to spend years getting good at it, hadn't you better enjoy it?

7. They are self-aware.

I am fortunate to work with a lot of impressive coaches and entrepreneurs at The Escape School and I am constantly struck by the extent to which they know what they like and don't like, what they are good at and what they aren't good at. As a result of clear self-knowledge, not only are they able to confidently accept or decline opportunities but they are also extremely aware of where their "edge" is and what their next challenge is. Knowing what the next step is on your own personal growth journey is extremely motivating.

8. *They find ways of being autonomous.*

Some of these same career coaches could be working in the corporate world, earning double what they earn from working with their individual clients. However, in order to do that they would have to compromise on a hell of a lot of things – location, hours, dress, subject matter, autonomy. Ultimately they would have to compromise their independence. I'm not saying that all of us should find ways of being sole traders or independent consultants. However, the more you can find ways of being more autonomous on the work front – even if you are fully employed by someone else – the more likely you are to enjoy your work.

9. *They act with integrity.*

For me, acting with integrity means acting in alignment with your values. It is so depressing hearing so many people talk about being pressured into doing things at work that go against their core values. I used to worry about what I might end up doing after Escape the City and whether I would find it fulfilling. However, I have now realised that as long as I am clear on what my values are, I can do pretty much anything, as long as it allows me to work hard on things that are aligned with my worldview and my principles.

People who do work they love have a clear mission. Avoid thinking about things like job titles, industries or professions. They all involve jumping through someone else's hoops or getting in someone else's box! Instead get clear on your WHY. Your WHY is your north star. This is the thing you'd do no matter what job title or what industry.

For example, my mission involves helping people challenge convention when convention is unhelpful to them. I am passionate about helping people get unstuck. I believe that the more people who are free to do work that matters to them, the better the world will be. I could do this in so many different ways – through coaching, writing, teaching, community building, event production, etc, etc.

My WHY doesn't align to a job title or even to an industry – it is the main thing that makes me tick and it is closely aligned with my core values.

I wasn't clear on my mission when I left my consulting job 5.5 years ago and started working on a wild idea to help people escape unfulfilling careers – I just followed my interests towards something that felt was worthwhile. Your mission can change as often as you need it to; it is constantly evolving. Pick something you know you care about and start doing it – you'll get all the information you need about your values and your mission through forward action.

10. *They have their own definition of success.*

Last but not least, people whose levels of work fulfilment are off the chart are usually those who have rejected the need for external validation and who are happy with having defined success for themselves. We live in a world where it is so easy to compare ourselves to other people and where we are constantly bombarded with cues as to what "success" is; status, money, power, possessions, seniority, etc. None of those things are inherently bad. The trap comes when we find ourselves playing someone else's game and chasing someone else's definition of success.

We need the courage to decide what we want in our lives and the determination to take one step after another (without knowing the end destination) in directions that we feel matter to us. No one who loves their work absolutely knew what it is that would truly make them tick before they started. The only difference between them and us is that they didn't let their doubts and unpreparedness stop them. They kept moving forwards until they found the thing that really made them tick, and then they doubled-down on getting damn good at it."

THE LEAN APPROACH TO CAREER DEVELOPMENT

Let's start with the idea that our minds run on software we create for it, based on data we've gathered from parents, teachers, peers, and so on. Lost graduates know that their scripts need a software update. Sometimes they go back and do yet another degree, and then graduate their masters' program feeling even more lost than before.

In tech, the old-school style of software development used a waterfall model, which is what it sounds like. It was linear and flowed in one direction – Stage 1 led to Stage 2, and so on. Similarly, this is how traditional education was arranged: you go to school, then college, then you get a job. This is the script behind our parents' advice. It was to adopt a waterfall method of software development.

These days, the world has become a lot more fluid: perhaps you go to school, then college, do an unpaid internship, find a job, complete another degree, take another job. You could have started out as a banker then trained as a nutritionist before taking a break from work in order to raise your first kid.

This means that the traditional organisation career, which was once perceived as the norm, is now seen by many career researchers as more relevant to the last century. In the future, we are likely to see careers characterised by flexible employment contracts, multiple employers, lateral job moves and multiple career changes – also known as the protean career, as described by career academic Stuart Hall:

"The protean career is a process which the person, not the organization, is managing [their career]… the criterion of success is internal (psychological success), not external."

This model emphasises taking responsibility for your own

career instead of relying on an employer to draft and map your career for you. It emphasises employability through embracing a lattice-like career of inter-organisational moves and life-long learning – as opposed to climbing a career ladder. The protean career is driven by personal career choices and a search for self-fulfilment.

We are no longer living in a world where the script behind your career "software" is best developed in a linear, logical "waterfall" fashion. Instead, the software behind your career best happens in an agile way, based on constant changes.

The "Lean Startup" movement is often linked to a book of the same name written by Eric Ries, inspired by the theories of Stanford professor Steve Blank. The "lean" methodology refers to a process where, instead of focusing on coming up with a business and then launching it to customers, you start with the people you're trying to help and define their pain before building anything.

Through a process known as "validated learning", you build a prototype, experiment using that prototype, and pivot towards a successful model. To pivot is to change, but to change according to data. This means a startup is built on data as opposed to a random hypothesis.

The career of any graduate is like a startup – the graduate does not yet have an established mode of earning revenue. Just like a startup is searching for a business model, so too are graduates still *searching* to earn money in the marketplace.

When applied to careers, taking a lean approach means approaching a career with an open mind and being willing to pivot when necessary. As Rob observed in his essay, what unites people who love do work they love often comes down to their approach, as opposed to their credentials. Taking a lean approach – or LEAN approach – means implementing strategic experimentation, as outlined below.

If you're a recent graduate, here is what I suggest based on years of helping people through the process at Escape the City:

LEARN

Getting an education and gaining a credential are no longer the same thing. Be prepared to start your own self-directed learning journey.

Adopt a supplier mindset
Think not about what the organisation can do for you, but what you can do for the organisation.

Focus on the compass
Instead of getting caught up with external markers of success, focus on psychological success.

Design your own curriculum
If you are moving into a new area, you're going to have to learn new information and skills – thanks to the web, you can now start learning a lot online.

EXPERIMENT

The best way to start figuring out what you might like to do is through actually doing a variety of things and observing the results.

Build your folio through a variety of organisations
It's hard to know what you might like to move into, so instead of forcing yourself to make big decisions overnight, start small with getting to know different organisations.

Take a deliberate pilgrimage
Travel can be a helpful tool in resetting and recalibrating yourself – travelling consciously and intentionally can be enormously useful in finding a new direction.

Execute a Minimum Viable Project
Instead of launching an entirely new career or business all at once, focus on setting yourself a small and manageable exercise that you can realistically accomplish.

ACHIEVE

Setting yourself goals and edging towards accomplishment helps to give structure and strategy to your experimentation.

Strengthen your strengths

Find out what your strengths are, or at least your strong interests, and let those guide you towards your next steps.

Refine your proximate objective
You don't need to figure out your grand plan all at once – all you need at this point is to start taking small steps. Set yourself the next small step.

Practice with an audience
Instead of working in isolation, make sure that you're including people in your plans wherever possible, as early on as you can.

NETWORK

Great opportunities come from meeting great people, and the best way to meet them is through becoming great at something yourself and then using your talent to help others.

Connect through contribution
The best place to start is through becoming a great team player

with a growth mindset, and focusing on how you can give something unique to your organisation and industry.

Approach mentors intelligently

Make it about them and not about you – if necessary, wait until you're in a strong position where reaching out to them allows you to provide value to them.

Create your own hub

Meet up regularly with like-minded allies who are on your wavelength and working on their own projects or careers in a similar way.

While the above are all practical in nature, I have also been fascinated by the broader context under which the LEAN framework sits. We are in the middle of a shift, not only when it comes to the way education is delivered, or how careers are constructed, but also the way in which this impacts how we relate to the world around us. Namely, the impact this has on identity, which I wanted to briefly explore in the following chapter.

[3]

FROM LOST TO LEAN

"We are not aligning the needs of the 21st century workforce with the skills we are teaching in our classrooms and that is a big mistake."

— *Fred Wilson*

Before he'd moved to Fiji, Andy had spent a couple of weeks working on a summer vacation placement at a small accounting firm near his hometown in England. He'd studied a general business management degree at university, so it hadn't seemed like a completely absurd suggestion that he'd wind up at a place like that, but after a few days, he knew that if this was his life for the next twenty years, he was out. It was a two-week placement.

On the final day, he told his parents that he was booking a one-way ticket to Fiji and he didn't look back. He hadn't learned much about business or accounting during his placement, but he had learned a number of things about himself. He didn't want to work behind a desk. He was going to have to figure out what to do with his time if he was going to course-correct the path that his degree had seemed to place him on.

He'd also learned an all-important lesson from his temporary boss, the owner of the company who had recently bought the firm off its founder, who winked at the butts of the secretaries who walked past and insisted that the interns addressed him as "Sir". Andy didn't want to spend his days, as he described to his friends, "Passively chained behind a desk, making a douchebag richer."

He had gotten through the last few days of the internship by pretending that he was a robot who simply needed to fulfil certain functions without having the capacity to emotionally react to anything going on.

What he loved about Fiji, beyond the sunshine and the sparkle of the place, was the sense that everyone seemed connected to one another. There was so much less bullshit here, he noticed. People smiled, and they meant it. They weren't robots; they were as far from robotic as he'd ever experienced. But it was like *Pleasantville* – this wasn't real life. This was his dream chapter before real life began.

When I met Andy, he had recently returned from Fiji, and was going through a phase where he was trying to figure out what was realistic, what was a fantasy, and what he was even looking for in the first place. I told him to be careful of sweeping assertions like "all accounting firms are boring" or "all travel leads to paradise" and so on.

What was interesting to me was the way that Andy epitomised what one of the earliest career counsellors, Frank Parsons, had talked about as far back as 1909:

"We guide our boys and girls to some extent through school, then drop them into this complex world to sink or swim as the case may be. Yet there is no part of life where the need for guidance is more emphatic than in the transition from school to work – the choice of a vocation, adequate preparation for it, and the attainment of efficiency and success. The building of a career is quite as difficult a problem as the building of a house, yet few ever sit down with pencil and paper, with expert information and counsel, to plan a working career and deal with the life problem scientifically, as they would deal with the problem of building a house, taking the advice of an architect to help them."

We often think that career dissatisfaction or career change is about switching jobs. It is actually about something much larger. It is about identity. Identity is the vehicle through which we experience the world, and with the advent of new technology and globalisation, questions of identity for today's millennials hold a different weight to what they held for our parents.

New Questions of Identity

The very essence of how millennials treat work is different to what it was for Baby Boomers. It is no longer about simply clocking in and making money.

For the specific subset of millennials who — by global standards — are well-educated and privileged enough to shoot for the higher end of Maslow's hierarchy of needs, work has become about self-actualisation, personal fulfilment, and a search for meaning.

Work has become an incredibly personal expression. You exchange your time for some kind of reward but what constitutes a meaningful reward is subjective.

I've noticed that if you have a job that is less traditional (e.g. Facebook Analytics Consultant) then of course it might seem less "real" to your parents. It represents labour on the more technologically progressive end of the spectrum, and anything progressive is often seen as less tangible than the established.

The traditional is more established. So when anyone asks if you're ever planning to get a "real" job what they are essentially questioning is whether you have the intention of entertaining a traditional route, which feels more tangible to them.

Now I understand that when anyone asks if you're going to get a "real" job, they're often saying, "Are you going to get a job that aligns to my values? Because my values determine my reality and your job matching my values therefore feels more tangible to me."

It was reassuring to me that even Ryan Avent, The Economist's senior economics editor and Free Exchange columnist, found a generational disconnect in communicating about work with *his* parents. He wrote a feature article titled, "*Why Do We Work So Hard?*", in which he explored how our jobs have become prisons which we don't want to leave. This, he says, is very different to our parents' experience of work.

He reflects that when his father had been a boy on the family farm, the tasks in the fields had been "gruelling and thankless". These days, things are different. The professional elite who get to solve complicated, interesting problems have the opportunity to engage in "fun" work – the challenge, he explains, is that it rarely stops. In a time of smartphones and the web, while software and information technology have taken away the drudgery of the workplace, they have also caused work to overshadow and merge with our identities as never before:

"The dollars and hours pile up as we aim for a good life that always stays just out of reach. In moments of exhaustion we imagine simpler lives in smaller towns with more hours free for family and hobbies and ourselves. Perhaps we just live in a nightmarish arms race: if we were all to disarm, collectively, then we could all live a calmer, happier, more equal life. But that is not quite how it is. The problem is not that overworked professionals are all miserable. The problem is that they are not."

He talks about how, for the previous generation, life happened outside of work – on holidays at the beach or volunteering or church. These days, he says, professionals with purpose find a great amount of pleasure in their day-to-day. He talks about the challenge of communicating this to his parents, where they see work as a job, and he sees work as the place where he constructs "identity, community, purpose – the things that provide meaning and motivation."

What Avent was also talking about was "flow", a mental state coined by psychologist Mihaly Csikszentmihaly to describe a pleasurable state of focused immersion in a challenging yet achievable task. Flow is what causes you to lose track of time through being highly engaged. When people talk about 'finding their passion' often they actually seem to be referring to finding the activity which puts them into a flow state, although the former rolls off the tongue much easier.

It is concepts like flow that are not covered in most education institutions, and this is what I personally struggle to understand. Instead, we cover topics like mitochondria and algebra and while these have their own functions, I can see how student disengagement happens. In an ideal world, each of us experiences a high level of engagement throughout our education journey so that we can go on to be great at whatever we end up choosing to pursue.

However, the current model does not set this up to be the case. That is why I am excited when I meet role models like Tom Rippin.

Future Education Models

I originally met Tom Rippin because I was as fascinated by his career trajectory as I was by the education model behind the social enterprise leadership development program On Purpose, which he founded and of which he is the current CEO.

How did Tom come to found and lead On Purpose? After some years researching cancer, Tom Rippin started his non-academic career at management consultants McKinsey & Company, where he worked across the private, public and non-profit sectors. He transitioned into the social enterprise space, first advising the CEO of Comic Relief on private sector matters and then working at RED, the business founded by Bono and Bobby Shriver to help eliminate AIDS in Africa, where he was Managing Director for Europe and Director of Business Development for RED International.

While On Purpose is defined as a social enterprise leadership training program, I believe it demonstrates the postgraduate university model of the future. It combines a four-day-a-week apprenticeship with a half-day of weekly training, in which each student gets matched with a coach or mentor, and gets paid while they complete the training. This blend of on-site training, high-quality peer support, mentoring and coaching, and teaching though practice instead of theory represents a new way of education through work placement.

This is the kind of education solution that would have helped lost graduates, as it removes a lot of the shame that comes with the Educational Ponzi Scheme. I thought of how Nadia had reported feeling: like *she* was an idiot for not knowing her passion, like *she* should feel extra ashamed for the privilege of doing an unpaid internship, like *she* was the problem.

The beauty about the On Purpose model is that it gives students more flexibility to find their own way while still providing a solid infrastructure of knowledge and contacts. After all, as we've explored, these days the questions of career construction are much more complex.

There are not only new questions of how to marry your interests with your pay cheque; there are also new issues around morality. When Andy told me that his Fijian experience had piqued his interest in working for the charity sector, I told him about *The Most Good You Can Do,* a book by philosopher Peter Singer.

Singer applauds earning gobs of money on Wall Street rather than being a social worker or even a medical doctor, provided you will donate most of your earnings to helping the poorest of the poor in the most cost-effective ways. He talks about Effective Altruism, a growing social movement that is about dedicating a significant part of one's life to improving the world and rigorously asking the question, "Of all the possible ways to make a difference, how can I make the greatest difference?"

I wanted the LEAN framework to help graduates match their day-to-day reality with the concepts like those talked about by Peter Singer, as well as those outlined by Priya Parker.

I hosted an Escape the City workshop with Parker in Manhattan. She is the founder of Thrive Labs. A conflict-resolution mediator by training, she has worked on peace processes in India, South Africa, Zambia and the Middle East, among other places. She is a co-founder of the Sustained Dialogue Campus Network, which works to improve inter-group relations at colleges and universities. She has also worked at the Dalai Lama's Foundation for Universal Responsibility, PRS Legislative Research in India, the White House Office of Social Innovation and Civic Participation, and the Omidyar Network.

A Phi Beta Kappa graduate of the University of Virginia, she holds dual master's degrees in business from the Massachusetts Institute of Technology and in government from the Harvard Kennedy School. She writes and speaks regularly about individual, organizational and societal change. I familiarised myself with her writing when I was preparing for the workshop we ran with her. One of the quotes I always loved from her epitomised what I had noticed in the many Escape members I had met to date:

"What I found was a rising generation of elite leaders who bring wonderful new gifts to the table – more empathy than their predecessors, more worldliness, more pragmatism for an angry, ideological age. But I also found my generation of young leaders paralyzed, hesitant, and unwilling stick their necks out and lead on the big questions of our time: how to build a more equitable and sustainable capitalism, how to manage the transition to a post-Western world, how to extend prosperity to developing countries without pushing the planet over the brink."

If we are going to grow or become those leaders, we need to go from the lost to the lean. But how? This is why I came up with the LEAN framework – I believe it starts with reprogramming our psychological make-up, instead of relying on the scripts we've been taught at school, or trying to buy another degree to give us the answers. There is no simple blueprint. As Tom Rippin himself said, he never began his journey with A Grand Plan All Mapped Out. I loved the advice he gave when I interviewed him for a Huffington Post piece.

"Beware the passion paralysis," he said. "When I was transitioning out of McKinsey, people said "just follow your passion" but this is not as easy as it seems! I still haven't figured out my "passion" – certainly not my life-long passion. Instead of trying to work out your passion, just figure out what you're going to do for the next 3 years and if that's sufficiently exciting to you, that's great. You can always change after 2-3 years."

What LEAN Cannot Cover

I noticed when sharing the LEAN framework that some Escape members seemed to be struggling with issues that were deeper than career transition. This was particularly obvious when I talked to those working in extremely high-pressure environments. I saw that what it takes to "succeed" in harsh work environments often goes against what it takes to develop positive mental health.

The lens through which I approached this was the book *Reinventing Your Life* by Jeffrey E. Young, Ph.D., and Janet S. Klosko, Ph.D. In this the authors explore schema therapy: a schema being the map through which we interpret reality. A maladaptive schema is one that is a toxic, unhelpful lens hat triggers depression and anguish.

Schemas can be understood as "broad, pervasive themes regarding oneself and one's relationship with others, developed during childhood and elaborated throughout one's lifetime, and dysfunctional to a significant degree."

I noticed that most of those people working in harsh environments tended to be overachievers. Through reading about schema therapy, I saw that the most common self-defeating emotional pattern affecting overachievers could be "Approval-Seeking" – a lens where excessive importance is placed on gaining recognition from others at the expense of building a secure and authentic sense of self.

This ties self-esteem to the reactions of others as opposed to one's innate inclinations. Sometimes this involves an overemphasis on achievement, status, or appearance as a means of winning admiration or attention, often prompting major life decisions that later feel unsatisfying or inauthentic, as well as causing a hypersensitivity to rejection.

Another schema I noticed among such Escape members was "Self-Sacrifice": "Excessive focus on voluntarily meeting the needs of others in daily situations, at the expense of one's own gratification." As well as "Emotional Inhibition": "The excessive inhibition of spontaneous action, feeling, or communication – usually to avoid disapproval by others, feelings of shame, or losing control of one's impulses."

Most of all, I noticed that while these two following schemas could be attributed to compromising an employee's mental health, it was a characteristic that corporate employers often actively looked for and encouraged in their employees. The first is "Unrelenting Standards" – "the underlying belief that one must strive to meet very high internalized standards of behavior and performance, usually to avoid criticism." The second is "Punitiveness" – "The belief that people should be harshly punished for making mistakes."

I could see that if Escape members had the above schemas only strengthened with each day that they remained in their jobs, they felt less resilient, and meant that whenever they even considered changing careers, they got too afraid. While I recommend the LEAN framework for those who are feeling pretty resilient already, I would suggest that if anyone was feeling the effects of depression or anxiety that they first work with a therapist. Having trained as a coach, I can also see that coaching is a powerful catalyst that can help strengthen your own experience of the LEAN principles.

But even without a coach or therapist, the LEAN principles can still be put into practice. This is what I remembered when

I spoke to Charlie, who still felt stuck within that grey zone between university and whatever came next. While he had spent hours frustrated at home, feeling trapped and powerless, it was during a party (where he was meant to be having fun) that he decided something needed to change.

[4]

LEARN

"The biggest thing is to not overcomplicate it and just start.
You don't have to have the whole thing mapped out. You don't
have to know where it's going to lead you. You shouldn't get
caught up in the results of it. You just need to begin and embrace
the journey and be open to where it's going to lead you."

— *Rich Roll*

It was only after he pressed the buzzer for 5A that Charlie double-checked his phone to make sure he had the right flat number. It was a Friday night and there was a group of his friends from university gathering at this girl Kelly's place. 5A, yes, he verified on the group email as the door made a buzzing sound and opened in front of him.

He climbed the stairs hoping that tonight's chat would focus on the usual bullshit instead of going into what everyone was doing and where everyone was working. He was starting to dread these group status updates as they only made him feel the same way as he did when he heard the sound of his parents shutting the door each weekday morning.

"Heeyyyyyyyyy!" Kelly said as she opened the door, dragging the word out for so long that Charlie could tell that the vodka soda in her hand was probably her fourth.

"How aaare you?" She drawled, leading him towards the living room where about ten familiar faces were perched around a coffee table littered with beer, vodka, and what seemed like a dozen half-empty glasses.

It was more of a statement than a question, Charlie realised, as Kelly quickly got distracted by her roommate Mariah interrupting her with a question about ice. A few hours later, after the bottles on the coffee table had become emptier and the music had become louder, Charlie watched his friends Marcus and Gill begin what looked a dance routine, but was actually Gill being forced to lie on the floor while Marcus tipped the bottle of beer into his mouth, causing hysterical fits of laughter all around.

These are the future leaders of Deloitte, Charlie thought. Or were they at Ernst & Young? He couldn't quite remember, even though Marcus had name-dropped the firm about a hundred times that night. Maybe Charlie's brain had switched off automatically and deliberately forgotten as a result.

Charlie looked around the room and realised that everyone there was either doing a corporate graduate scheme for a well-known brand, still studying, had just come back from travelling or was about to go abroad. He took a sip of his beer, hoping to get drunk faster. As he watched Gill stand up off the floor with his shirt half-wet and his face scrunched with laughter, Charlie realised that in more ways than one that evening, he already felt left behind.

It was a few days later that Charlie came to an Escape the City event, even though he wasn't technically the target audience. He didn't even have any work experience, he reminded me, but he had come because a friend at that party had recommended he check it out. Something about the party had made him reflect, he said – looking around the room, he said that a year from now, he didn't want to be the only one of his friends who had nothing to show for his year.

As he described his day-to-day of sending out hundreds of applications and hearing nothing back, I noted the dejection he was trying to hide in his voice.

"I can tell you're feeling kind of helpless," I observed.

"Well, I'm just not sure what I'm meant to do?" Charlie said. "I'm sending out stuff, hearing nothing back… I don't want to travel, I've done that. I'm just not sure where to start." It was when he started talking about how he felt like he was setting himself up for long-term failure that I almost shushed him, but restrained myself.

"You're stressing out about the next 30 years, when really, you just need to focus on the next few months," I said. "Trust me, most people I know felt the exact same way when they left university."

I tried to choose my words carefully. "Treat this period less like an extended holiday at your parent's place, and more like a self-directed master's program, where you get to build the curriculum, without having to go into any debt."

Charlie smirked. I told him that the last thing anyone wants to do when they leave university is more studying, but that there is a strong difference between cramming for an exam because you have to get a certain grade, and becoming immersed in a subject you are genuinely interested in.

"The trouble is," I said to him. "I bet you're not even sure what you're interested in." And that's where we need to start, I told him.

The LEAN framework: Learn

Charlie hadn't been a terrible student, but he hadn't exactly been a stellar one either. He had chosen to muck around with mates instead of doing any internships during university. He had worked a couple of menial jobs for the cash but he didn't see how lawn-mowing and scooping ice cream was going to set him up for a future career.

I told him that the approach that most graduates take after university is fairly reactive. They apply to the jobs they see advertised but they have no idea about the jobs that aren't advertised. They treat a corporate training program as if there is a teacher grading them, and sometimes there are peers ranking them and feeding back on their behaviour, which only reinforces the sheep mentality.

"If you want to 'do something different,'" I said, quoting Escape the City's tagline, "You have to think a little differently to how most graduates think." That comes down to exploring the following principles, which I explained to Charlie through the lens of my own experiences:

- **Adopt a supplier mindset** – When I left university, I assumed that I had to have a certain qualification or piece of paper to get certain companies to talk to me. Later, I found out that often, at least when it came to smaller businesses, all I needed was a game plan to help them grow. When companies interested me, I approached them with a specific plan of how I could help them on a short-term project. This sometimes led to paid work, and sometimes it was a short-term volunteer gig. Often it fell outside of my day job at the time, which was my main source of income.

- **Focus on the compass** – Instead of trying to figure everything out, and see what my friends were doing, and comparing myself to them, I tried as often as possible to shift the focus on how I felt about what I was doing and whether or not it felt right to me. I tried to focus on the next few steps ahead, instead of trying to predict the next twenty years at a time.

- **Design your own curriculum** – Even though I've been in marketing for almost a decade, I still take online courses and I don't think I'll ever stop doing this. Sometimes I'll teach workshops and sometimes I'll be in the student's seat. I think that finding a career you love has to start with wanting to find out as much information as possible around that subject area. Staying engaged with what you do comes down to wanting to learn as much as possible about the area you work in.

"That sounds great in theory," Charlie said. "But I'm not sure how to actually go about doing it." So we sat down and went through each point in detail.

Adopt a Supplier Mindset

When you're a kid, your parents are there to serve you. Are you happy? Are you fed? Are you clothed? Are you dressed for school? It's all about you. At school, your teachers are there to serve you and make sure that you pass. Are you studying? Did you do your homework? It's all about you.

After you leave school, it's not about you any more. Nobody really cares whether you're happy or not. If you're not fed or dressed, that's your problem. And if you want to work for someone, you had better start thinking with a supplier mindset instead of a customer mindset.

A big issue with graduates is when they expect to be served like customers. If they expect their boss to serve as their parent or their teacher, they're going to be sorely disappointed. The boss is there to run an organisation. If you can make your boss's job easier, they're going to want to make your life easier.

The most effective graduates and colleagues see themselves as suppliers. They've asked themselves what their organisation or boss needs and they've worked hard to deliver it for them. It's easy to forget your ego when you're connected to that mindset because it is not about you. It's about supplying the business with what it needs and supplying your boss with what they need.

"You know, there is a great book called *So Good They Can't Ignore You* by Cal Newport," I told Charlie. "You should check it out." The most important thing he says is this: "Building valuable skills is hard and takes time. For someone in a new position, the right question is not, "What is this job offering me?" but, instead, "What am I offering this job?"

Newport talks about the supplier mindset without referring to it as such. He explains how millennials are preoccupied with discovering their passion when actually, commitment first is what leads to competence. Competence leads to engagement. And engagement leads to "flow" (which we often mistakingly refer to as "passion" as we explored earlier on).

Someone who demonstrated this mindset, I told Charlie, was a family friend of mine, Julien, who had no idea what he wanted to do after university. Before he started following a supplier mindset, he first stumbled through "researching" as many jobs as possible to figure out what might be a good fit. He searched online, looked at job descriptions and requirements and maybe googled what it was like to work in a particular job. He didn't speak to anyone, didn't hold any information interviews. He had no idea what he was doing.

As a last resort he went to his network ("I should have done this first!" he later said) and reached out for possible internships. He got one at Done and Dusted, a TV production company in London. He wound up spending two years in the industry and had a fair amount of success working as a freelancer but finally decided it wasn't for him.

He started doing deep research into what he wanted to do and decided to become a coach. Things started off well but then he found out he was expecting a daughter, and needed a stable income fast. He ended up working for his father at his Medical Insurance business a few months later. He has been there ever since and his career has sky rocketed (not because of family ties) and a new passion for business has developed.

I had seen Julien start as a project coordinator and in the last 18 months, he moved up to Assistant Operations Manager, Development Projects Manager and finally Operations Manager. He is now set to become the General Manager in the next year.

A well-known blogger called Ramit Sethi, whose story we will explore further on in the chapter, has an online course called the Dream Job program. Julien completed this and attributes everything that he's learned to that program. The program helped him to triple his rates as a freelancer in television production and to multiply his salary by five times in less than two years.

When I asked Julien about the practicalities of operating with a supplier mindset in the early stages of job-hunting, he offered the following advice, which I reported back to Charlie:

"Whatever job you go after, make sure your decision is backed by solid research. Connect with people who have the jobs you think you want, take them out to coffee, get on a Skype call with them and learn the details about their job. What's it like day to day, how did they get there, what are the most important skills to learn, what are the career progression options and so on.

Then start to look for companies you want to work for. Again, speak to people who are either working there now or worked there previously. Find out everything you can, what the leadership team is like, what are their biggest challenges, where is the company headed in the next five years? Really try to understand the company.

By this point, you should have an idea of what job you want and the top three to five companies you're interested in. Now it's time to prepare your Cover Letter and CV. Make sure there's a narrative in your CV and cover letter. Use the language of the company you're applying to as it will resonate with the hiring manager. Since you already know people at the company, you should be able to get your CV to the top of the pile for an interview.

Once you have an interview the real work starts. Practice, practice, practice. Go through standard interview questions and practice answering them. Even better, get a friend to help and record yourself. You'd be surprised what you can learn from watching yourself back.

To really dominate an interview, prepare a detailed document explaining the company that you're pitching, the challenges they are facing and exactly what you can do to overcome them. You'll instantly put yourself in the top performer bracket if you can do this. Why? Because 99% of people aren't willing to put this amount of effort in."

It was this last point that I thought particularly demonstrated the supplier mindset in practice. A lot of people go into a job with a customer mindset – what can this job give me? What can this employer give me? While it's important to know your own expectations, you are much more likely to increase your employability prospects by putting the organisation's needs first and asking yourself; what does this organisation need? What can I give it? How can I help this organisation get stronger?

FOCUS ON THE COMPASS

When we graduate from formal education, we leave behind a familiar system. We also leave the safety nest of our parents' home and our college social circle. It is a crucial time in our life where we transition from adolescence into adulthood. The definition of adulthood, as I saw it, is making up your own mind about things – deciding who you want to become (not who your parents, peers, society, and so on, expect you to be).

Part of this involves improving the way you communicate with yourself and navigate your choices. I noticed certain friends asking themselves tough questions about whether they were actually enjoying themselves or whether they were simply drifting along with their peers, not really sure what they truly wanted from their careers.

Besides Julien's story, I also told Charlie about Alex O'Byrne, who runs We Make Websites.

We Make Websites is now the highest rated Shopify agency in the UK with over 300 projects completed and 40,000 retailers reading their advice each month. Clients include Condor bikes and The Economist and two businesses that are in startup finals for Virgin and Shopify.

But five years ago, Alex did not leave his job at Merrill Lynch and decide he was going to be the number one rated Shopify agency.

When Alex started looking for internships after university, he had no idea what he wanted to do. He just wanted to feel like he was "going places".

"At that time in computer science, startups weren't really a big thing, a legitimate career path, whereas I think they are now," Alex says. "The only people recruiting were banks and they were paying well back in 2006. Most offered graduates a few months in New York having fun, er, training... so I did this but soon after the glory days of training, I realised a corporate job wasn't for me."

He didn't enjoy it as there was "limited ability to actually make a difference, bad software, politics, long decision cycles, ugly offices, having a boss... and all the time I knew I could be making better technology with new tools and a fresh mindset."

The problem was knowing what to do, and at the time the easiest thing was to create a web agency, helping people out. After messing around making apps and pitching for a big website project and getting to second place, he and his business partner Piers (who he had met at Merrill Lynch) had registered and set up a business in a week.

Alex then went on an "one of those epiphany holidays in Nice" and on the day he returned, he quit, called Piers and told him the news. The business grew slowly. Eventually, he decided to have a career break and spent three months driving around in a camper van in Eastern Europe with his girlfriend. Then he went to South America and by the end of that was ready to come back and switch it up a gear.

The big change was when he and Piers switched so that he focused on marketing and working "on" the business. Alex focused on e-commerce and then Shopify, and that is when things picked up.

Reflecting, Alex said: "The big corporate experience was useful for learning to be professional (soft skills) and how to do engineering 'properly' – for example, smooth releases."

"In university, I just didn't seem to question joining a large company, it seemed like that's what successful people did. I now notice that for many talented people there are other options they could consider, including startups. This was brought about by mainstream acceptance of startups such as Airbnb, Uber, Facebook and Spotify."

When I asked Alex about his advice for graduates, a lot of it was around trusting yourself that, in the long run, you will know what is best for you. Alex said:

- "It could be worth trying to get at least one well-known company on your CV as it can open doors and makes you look more trustworthy."
- "Five years seems like forever when you're in your early 20s but trust me, it's not. Some people even change careers every five years. So, build in time to travel or do whatever it is that you define as 'freedom'."
- "Make plans but be willing to change them. Do favours as it's nice and it may come back to help you one day."
- "Consider living abroad early on as it really does get harder with time."
- "Don't worry too much about the future, we all adapt and things have a habit of working out."

"I like that Alex consistently made choices that strengthened his own inner compass," I said to Charlie. "When it was time to leave Merill, he left. When it was time for him to go travelling, he did. Now they're the top Shopify agency in the UK. But that wasn't necessarily the goal when he left the corporate world – I mean, was Shopify even around when he left Merrill? Things change so fast."

"So what you're saying," Charlie paused. "Is that it's not about plotting where to go in 30 years, it's about getting good at something now, in this moment, then seeing where it takes you in the next few years." I nodded.

Design Your Own Curriculum

Now that Charlie seemed more ready to engage with the world, we talked about the importance of him setting his own learning journey out.

"Instead of sending out countless letters to companies, each day should be seen as a chance to learn something new," I said to him. I told him what I look for when I'm hiring.

"It's easy to hire for competence, but you can't *give* someone passion," I explained. "Ideally, I hire for both passion and competence, but if I have to pick, I choose to hire someone who's got passion and enjoys learning new things. At this age, you're too young to be indispensably competent yet. So you've got to be indispensably passionate."

"But what if I don't know what I'm passionate about?" Charlie asked.

"I think it starts with being interested in something first," I said. "Something you'll never get sick of learning about."

"Where would I learn, though?" Charlie asked.

"Read some blogs. Start a blog. Watch YouTube. Go to events. You can have heroes and mentors, you don't need to meet them in real life to have sort of a relationship with them. You can read their stuff, learn their lessons, and so on."

As Alex had said himself once: "Learn, learn, learn... whether that's online communities, reading, podcasts – stay on top of your subject area."

I told Charlie that about an entire ecosystem of well-known bloggers who we had the chance to learn from at Escape the City. Some figures to learn from included the below list:

- **Ramit Sethi** – Bestselling author who has taught thousands to manage their personal finances. You can read more at www.iwillteachyoutoberich.com

- **Pamela Slim** – Award-winning author, speaker and business consultant with a passion for career and organizational development. You can read her blog here: www.pamelaslim.com/blog

- **Tim Ferriss** – Author, entrepreneur, angel investor, and public speaker. He has written a number of self-help books and you can read his blog here: http://fourhourworkweek.com/blog/

- **Chris Guillebeau** – Best known for The Art of Non-Conformity blog and book. He has also written guides for travel and small business topics under the brand Unconventional Guides. He organizes the annual World Domination Summit in Portland, Oregon. His website is here: http://chrisguillebeau.com/

- **Seth Godin** – Author, entrepreneur, marketer, and public speaker who riffs on marketing, respect, and the ways ideas spread here: http://sethgodin.typepad.com/

- **Paul Graham** – Well-known programmer, writer, and investor. Started Y Combinator, which has funded over 1000 startups, including Dropbox, Airbnb, Stripe, and Reddit. His essays are here: http://paulgraham.com/articles.html

- **James Altucher** – American hedge fund manager, entrepreneur, bestselling author, and podcaster. His website is http://www.jamesaltucher.com/

While the above are by no means an exhaustive list, it would be entirely possible to spend many, many hours immersing yourself in the writings of those featured above. Since bloggers are like television shows, in that each person's taste is extremely personal, I didn't feel like it was my place to tell Charlie who he should be following. I simply gave him the list and told him to explore them all.

There are also the following websites which I suggested Charlie check out:

- **Udemy** – an online learning marketplace, where 10 million+ students are taking courses in everything from programming to yoga to photography and much, much more. Each of the 40,000+ courses is taught by an expert instructor, and every course is available on-demand, so students can learn at their own pace, on their own time, and on any device.

- **Coursera** – an education platform that partners with top universities and organizations worldwide, to offer courses online for anyone to take.

Again, the usefulness of the above websites would be determined by what Charlie specifically wanted to learn and how much time he had available.

SUMMARY

Essentially, I told Charlie, adopting a supplier mindset involved thinking about the organisations he wanted to target and putting their needs before his ego. Much like Julien demonstrated, committing to an organisation builds competence, which builds engagement, which often leads to a higher salary in the long run.

Focusing on the compass, as Alex had shown, meant calibrating the internal compass so that even if you were travelling or taking a career break or deciding to switch organisations, you were tuning into what was best for you, instead of taking cues from peers or parents.

Designing your own curriculum meant setting aside time to explore the topics that were interesting. There are a plethora of resources online about any area that might interest you.

I told Charlie to keep in touch. A few days later, I found myself having a similar conversation with Sam. Although she was in a different position to Charlie, in that she already had a job as a management consultant, she was facing her own set of issues about breaking up with her career.

[5]

EXPERIMENT

"So long as your desire to explore is greater than your desire to not screw up, you're on the right track. A life oriented toward discovery is infinitely more rewarding than a life oriented toward not blowing it."

— *Ed Helms*

Sam wanted to do something more creative but she wasn't quite sure where to start. Sometimes she felt it with piercing clarity and other times it played in the background soundtrack of her mind on soft volume. On weeks when she was particularly frustrated, she'd sit with her friends and toss around ideas about businesses they could start or alternative paths they could pursue. While she spent a lot of time in Kuala Lumpur, this month she was back in Manhattan.

There was one particular day where she found herself arguing with her boyfriend at 5:45am over the "noise" she was making as she got ready for work. "You're being so loud," he groaned. She tried to move around more silently. She was at the office by 6:30am in order to finish an Excel model that her boss had requested in her inbox by 8:00am. She yawned as she clicked the keyboard, wishing that she had more than a vending machine coffee and a granola bar as breakfast.

Her boss had ended up not even needing the Excel model, and had come by her desk at 10:30am to tell her that she'd need to stay late that day in order to be part of a conference call at 8:00pm. As Sam texted her boyfriend cancelling that night's dinner reservations, she internally cringed in advance, knowing that he would be adding this to the mental tally he seemed to be keeping of times when she "put her career before what really mattered." He was a web designer with much more reasonable hours and he often acted like she was having an affair with her job behind his back.

Once, she even went so far as to look up yoga teacher training in Costa Rica. Her mouse hovered over the "enrol" button, picturing morning sunshine and walks on the beach. She would be as far away from this world of Powerpoint decks and Excel models as possible. But then her phone beeped with a Whatsapp message, the dream faded, and she closed down the windows, returning back to her spreadsheet.

Sam recounted the above to me when I was in New York for an Escape event. As she lamented her lack of awareness around her own passions as if it were a lack of ability or something she should just automatically know, I immediately thought of a New York Times piece titled, *"It's Not About You"* written by David Brooks.

Brooks talks about how we live in this era "that preaches the self as the centre of a life." To follow your passion, your dream, your "true self", the common assumption is that you have to first figure out "you" and then build a life around that.

Instead, Brooks says, you don't find much by introspection in itself – rather: "Most people don't form a self and then lead a life. They are called by a problem, and the self is constructed gradually by their calling." When we make a meaningful contribution, we feel validated.

People want to feel like they matter, that by getting out of bed, someone noticed; that something changed because they existed. But that only happens when we figure out where our time belongs.

Brooks says the problem is that college grads are perpetually told this story of "limitless possibilities" when really, success in young adulthood means the start of making "sacred commitments — to a spouse, a community and calling." The world that college graduates now enter is more unstructured than ever before – and we have to create our own navigational skills.

Instead of trying to figure out her "true self" and therefore her next career move as a short-term and independent decision, I told Sam that maybe it would be more productive to treat it as a long-term and interdependent process. The best place to start, I advised, would be with experimentation.

The LEAN framework: Experiment

One of the stories I pointed Sam towards was that of Allison Baum, who is now a Managing Partner at Fresco Capital, who are early stage venture investors supporting exceptional entrepreneurs. She is based in Tokyo.

How did she get there? Not by shifting overnight: after graduating from Harvard, Allison worked in Manhattan, first at Goldman Sachs and then at global educational company General Assembly in Manhattan. She then launched General Assembly in Hong Kong, before moving to Fresco Capital in Hong Kong. She now works at Fresco Capital in Tokyo.

She described her days at Goldman Sachs similar to how Sam talked about her own workday:

"A typical day at work started with copious amounts of caffeine at 6 am, followed by co-workers putting their feet up on their desks, drinking Monster energy drinks and taking prescription drugs. There was a lot of shooting the shit with clients on the phone and screaming at traders or brokers for (debatably) messing something up. There were plenty of mini footballs being thrown around the trading floor, and superiors would regularly motivate people by employing frat-boy antics that were centred around challenging people to improve by constantly putting them down in front of others. Then, we'd often end the day with drinks and fancy dinners in Midtown."

Allison didn't get from that scenario to where she is now, I told Sam, by suddenly quitting her job without a plan. Instead, she stayed open and flexible enough, yet strategic and deliberate enough, to surf the delicate balance between exploration and commitment. I led Sam through the following principles I had seen in practice through Allison's story, and those of others who had also left corporate jobs in pursuit of more meaning:

- **Build your folio through a variety of projects** – Allison did not decide overnight to work as an investor. Instead, over a few years, she took various projects and roles with different organisations to build up her experience. The best people, a mentor once told me, are T-shaped – they have a broad range of general skills but expertise in one specific area. Allison, to me, has built up this kind of T-shaped career.

- **Take a deliberate pilgrimage** – A lot of people use travel as a tool to give themselves a break from daily routine and some time and space to reflect. Someone who used long-term travel to shift his career is Matt Trinetti, whose story we explore in this chapter. Matt practices the art of deliberate travel, which is travelling consciously and using the time wisely, instead of getting wasted with random backpackers and then returning home finding yourself more broke and confused than before.

- **Execute a Minimum Viable Project** – I once heard a startup founder say, "Life is too short to do things you suck at. Focus on your strengths and on improving your weaknesses to the point where they don't hold you back. Don't try to correct all your weak points." Sometimes the only way to find out what our strengths are is to test them and put them into practice, which we don't necessarily have to do by switching roles entirely. We can take on projects and test our way towards what works.

Build Your Folio Through a Variety of Projects

A folio, I explained to Sam, is shorthand for "portfolio", the body of work that you've built up over your career. CVs explore the roles you've had but with certain careers, employers care less about what you've done and more about what you can do for them in the future.

For instance, I told Sam, when I hired a filmmaker on a previous project I worked on, I cared less about what his CV said and more about the videos he had actually produced. Similarly, when I'm interviewing graduates, I care less about their CVs and more about the projects they've worked on, with which companies or volunteer organisations, and so on.

As Seth Godin said, "The future is about gigs and assets and art and an ever-shifting series of partnerships and projects. It will change the fabric of our society along the way." While we've already explored the concept of the protean career, another word for it that's often thrown around is the idea of the "portfolio" career. Allison is a great example of someone who used each of her previous experiences to leverage herself to the next, and now she has a body of work spanning two continents, various organisations, and a wide range of financial areas.

She went from Harvard to Goldman to General Assembly in New York to General Assembly in Hong Kong to Tokyo. She built her portfolio though a variety of networks, and it began when she was working at Goldman.

While she was still at Goldman, Allison did some volunteer work with a woman who was involved in microfinance and was making a documentary about it. She helped her with production and marketing logistics, and it was through that woman that she got introduced to General Assembly in New York.

At General Assembly in New York, Allison was in charge of building out, launching, and growing part-time and full-time programs training professionals in digital skills that can help them pursue work that they love. It was when her boyfriend at the time got transferred to Hong Kong that she approached her bosses at General Assembly and asked to lead the Hong Kong office.

She eventually grew the Hong Kong arm into a profitable venture in its own right, and she did it because she knew how to hustle. As I showed Sam from Allison's blog, Allison had a spirit that you just can't buy. She made the most of each of her days there. As she writes:

"I feel like I'm on a scavenger hunt. Since I arrived here, I've been reaching out to people throughout Hong Kong that are involved in the entrepreneurial scene in one or way or another. One of the reasons why I am slowly falling in love with this city is that all of these people have e-mailed me back. What is that?! In New York, maybe I'm just particularly annoying but I have found that cold e-mails get <50% response rate, even if they are flattering to the recipient.

Once I'm over the shock of actually receiving a response, I arrange to meet with them, whether it be for a quick coffee, lunch, or just plain old conversation. When this process begins, I glance at my empty calendar to suggest a time and carefully concoct a way of not sounding too pathetic with my lack of plans. Then, before I know it, someone else e-mails back. I arrange a meeting, spending less time on not sounding pathetic since now I actually have something else on my calendar. Rinse, repeat until calendar is completely full."

She went for a lot of coffees and meetings, not necessarily knowing where they were all going to lead. These meetings are often what led to further introductions, which led to projects, which eventually led to the various roles she's had over the years, as well as the conferences she has spoken at.

"I just think I'd be too nervous to take that approach," Sam confessed.

"Why?" I asked.

"I'd assume things wouldn't work out, I guess," Sam continued.

After speaking to Sam about her tendency to expect the worse to happen, I told her to read *Learned Optimism* by Martin Seligman, a 1990 book that includes excellent advice on adjusting your explanatory style.

Optimism is not positive thinking, insists Seligman. It is avoiding negative thinking during setbacks. He introduces various concepts that help us understand his view on optimism, but the one I wanted to focus on was explanatory style – the method we can use to explain to ourselves why things happen, how it is not our fault and how we are still in control. There are three aspects to adjusting your explanatory style:

Permanence: If you believe that bad things that happen are permanent, that the suffering is everlasting, and that you will never be able to climb out of the hole, this is a pessimistic outlook. It will define your motivation to get back on your feet after a setback. Optimistic people see bad events to be more temporary setbacks. They point to specific temporary causes for negative events; pessimists point to permanent causes.

Pervasiveness: Pessimistic people assume that failure in one area of life means overall failure in life. Optimistic people compartmentalise the setback to the particular area in which the event occurred. Optimists believe the suffering is specific, as opposed to universal.

Personalisation: Pessimists blame themselves for events that occur whereas optimists blame bad events on causes outside of themselves. Optimists internalise positive events; pessimists externalise them.

Even the most optimistic person in the world will feel temporarily helpless when there is failure but optimism is not about never feeling bad – it is about learning to feel better, faster. The way I interpret Seligman's teaching is that if we want to increase our capacity for learned optimism, we need to treat setbacks as temporary, specific, and beyond our control. What we can determine is how we respond to them.

Like Allison, this means that when you move to a new city, start out in a new job or industry, begin a new business, or anything beyond your comfort zone, you learn not to treat any setbacks as permanent, pervasive, and personal. Allison rose through the ranks of Asia's venture capital scene because she was not only specific and focused in what she was learning about but also adopted an optimistic outlook every time she experienced a setback.

Take a Deliberate Pilgrimage

While Sam wasn't sure if she wanted to move countries like Allison did, because her boyfriend was based in New York, I told her about Matt Trinetti, who had negotiated a sabbatical instead of quitting his job entirely. This brought me onto the subject of travel, and specifically, long-term travel – which I have had mixed feelings about.

I have seen many Escape members use travel as a tool to reset themselves in between switching chapters in their lives. I have also read a lot of travel blogs not only from the Escape members but also from high-profile bloggers such as Nomadic Matt (who shares the same first name as Matt Trinetti, but is a different blogger). I can completely relate to the hunger for new experiences and the appeal of a location-independent lifestyle – personally, I grew up between the skyscrapers of Hong Kong, the rolling fields of New Zealand and the baking heat of Malaysia – so the nomadic lifestyle is something I was born into.

As a result, I've always made travel a priority in my life. I remember swimming in Maui, sunbathing in Sydney, and feeling weirdly connected to everything around me. In those moments, everything has been perfect. It's a thrilling calm that puts life into technicolor – when floating in crystal-clear water, or staring at the stars, there's almost a spiritual crescendo that insulates you from any worries and stress – you're trapped in the moment, this moment, and nothing can touch you here. So I understand why travel can be such a tempting drug.

However, I have also seen travel used as a means of avoiding real life. Anyone who believes that you can just buy a plane ticket, and with that, buy a new life, and with that, a new confidence, forgets that no matter where you go, you carry the same issues with you. Changing your postcode, your 'location' online, how things look to others – easy. Looking within yourself, changing behaviours, building a career where you already are – much more challenging.

This is why I admire Matt Trinetti's approach of *deliberate* travel, where travel is a conscious means of switching gears in your life. Matt himself explains his own long-term trip, which he refers to as a pilgrimage, on his personal blog GiveLiveExplore.com:

"Travel had always been a big part of my life, but the neatly partitioned two-week vacations never seemed to satisfy my wanderlust. I always wanted to travel long-term and explore the world at my own pace, to experience life in the most stripped-down and honest sense of the word.

Like many others my age, I had dreams of travelling around the world. But as my career as an IBM consultant grew, the timing never seemed perfect. Four years later, I was still working and still dreaming.

On January 17, 2012 everything changed. While sitting in an uninspiring client meeting, I received a call that my friend Shannon died unexpectedly in a car accident while driving home from work the night before.

As I mourned and celebrated her life, I reflected upon my own mortality, my potential regrets, and unrealized dreams. I finally confronted the fact that instead of living deliberately, I had mostly been going through the motions of life — accepting that life was meant to be lived a certain way, without thinking much about the why. In that moment, I resolved not to squander any more of my brief time on earth living a life that didn't suit me. And suddenly, that dream of world travel seemed a lot more urgent.

The next week, I booked a one-way ticket to Iceland, departing in six months. I wasn't sure what I would do about my job, my apartment in Chicago, my things, or my responsibilities.

But I had the simple confidence that things would work out."

And indeed they did work out. Matt went on to work with Escape the City, give a TED talk which was viewed by over 25,000 people, and write for the New York Observer, Virgin, among other publications. His Medium pieces have been shared by Arianna Huffington.

While this is one way to approach a pilgrimage, another example I told Sam about was that of Joanne Gan, who was also living in New York, and working in finance. She had studied economics and international relations at university and wanted to learn more about international development and work in the development field.

She knew that field experience (in developing countries) was a must – both because it was something she had always wanted to do personally, but also because she knew that to really understand development issues, it was important to work in the field and experience things first-hand.

Joanne did a three month placement in Indonesia for Kiva and for her second placement, she chose to stay in the Southeast Asia region and go to a large micro-finance institution in the Philippines. Spending time in both countries, she developed a deeper knowledge of Southeast Asia which (while she didn't know it at the time) helped her further her career as she later went on to manage the SE Asia portfolio at Kiva.

When Joanne did her travel, this fixed short-term commitment to being overseas also allowed her to take a sabbatical — which was a large plus as firstly, she had a job to return to and secondly, she did not risk losing her work status in the USA. As I explained

to Sam, not all travel stories had to involve quitting your job –
a sabbatical was often a great way to test out life in another
country or industry or both.

Joanne's twin sister, Rachael, also took a pilgrimage of her own.
She had worked an intense job in the finance industry for about
8 years, before deciding that finance might not be what she
wanted to pursue long-term, and that now was the time to try
something different and more entrepreneurial. She decided to
travel for six months to a year.

"I knew that now was the chance to seize the opportunity to
travel, when I had no responsibilities like a mortgage or family,"
she says. "I had a broad idea that post-travel, I would relocate
from New York to London and work in the startup sphere, but I
was willing to see where the journey would lead."

"Post-travel, I've decided to spend the next year in London
working on early stage startups — including my own," she
shares. "I'm an advisor to a philanthropic advisory tech startup,
co-founder of a new London social enterprise focused on food
surplus, and trying to launch another startup with a friend
around job search."

"I'm not sure which, if any, of these will become a full-time path
– they're all part-time roles currently, though there is potential
for the second and third to grow into something much larger.
Life post-travel is still very much a flexible path."

Rachael talks about how travel helped her to reset: "When in the
finance world, I got used to a certain lifestyle, but now I know
that that lifestyle is not what I need to get by – I can quite easily
get by on less money."

I told Sam how Rachael had spent a month working for a woman
who runs guesthouses in rural France, doing cooking, gardening,

cleaning in exchange for room and board. She met some of the guests, one of whom was from a client firm of her old bank.

"There was recognition that a job gave you a certain status in life," Rachael reflects. "But I guess when confronted with it from a different angle, my experience makes you re-evaluate how much that status means to you."

"I think, for any individual, going on an adventure and traveling on your own will give you a new type of confidence," she concludes. "While I didn't travel on my own for an entire year, I did stints on my own – trying new experiences, meeting new people, talking about new ideas in different settings has given me greater confidence and a greater sense of self."

"It sounds cheesy but it's true," she says. "I don't have it all figured out from that travel stint, but I can without a doubt say I feel more confident – it could just be age that's done that too."

I pointed out to Sam that travel is largely a personal journey. I also added that a trip did not necessarily have to be long-term to be effective. I remembered the story of Frank Yeung, who had been working at Goldman Sachs and took a two-week holiday in order to reflect deeply on what he wanted to do long-term. He returned from the holiday and went in to quit the day he got back. Not all stories about travel end with a resignation, but changing environments physically can certainly make a huge difference.

Execute a Minimum Viable Project

The "minimum viable" is a lean startup term and it refers to the seed, or the prototype version, of a product. Since we live in an age where we can build apps quickly and cheaply – a tester product (the "minimum viable") allows a startup to launch, tweak, refine, before investing large sums into scaling up. Similarly, a Minimum Viable Project refers to the idea that you can dip your toes into a potential career without necessarily handing in your notice.

"Would a pilgrimage be an example of a Minimum Viable Project?" Sam asked.

"Yes, depending on whether you're actually getting stuff done or not," I replied. "Joanne did her Kiva fellowship. Rachael took on various projects while she was abroad, with the startups she now works with. Matt did various projects for Escape the City while he was on his travels – he would often deliver a blog post or a talk, and that is what introduced him to the organisation that he now works at full-time."

Sam sighed. Then she said carefully, "I'm just not sure if what I'm interested in could be tested out without me making more space in my life for it."

"I see what you're saying," I replied. "But what's the alternative? If you don't quit your job or change the way things are at work, you're going to keep feeling dissatisfied. If you quit your job but have nothing else lined up, you might feel even more listless. So the balance might be making more time, however you can, whether that's evenings or weekends, to follow what's interesting to you."

When I asked Sam about the areas she was interested in, she mentioned yoga. In an ideal world, she would train as a yoga teacher for teenagers, she said, and set up her own yoga studio for teenage girls with eating disorders. "Simplify, simplify, simplify," I told her. "What's a smaller step?" After I repeatedly quizzed her on the simplest possible execution of this idea, she decided that she could run a yoga session in the park for teenage girls in her network, and then go from there.

Summary

"So I guess I don't just have to quit my job overnight," Sam remarked. I shrugged, thinking of Escape members in the past who had done just that.

"I think things have a way of working out, regardless," I said to her. "But personally, I think it's worth building your portfolio as much as possible while you're still in the safety of employment. Travel can be amazing and there are so many ways to do it – taking a sabbatical is great way to mitigate your risks. And focusing on projects, instead of forcing yourself to come up with an entirely new role in a new sector where you don't yet have contacts, is much more manageable."

"My boyfriend will be happy," Sam smiled. "I think he was scared I was going to run away to Costa Rica and become a yoga teacher by the ocean."

[6]

ACHIEVE

"To achieve something of significance, you have to give up things of inconsequence. This is hardly an astute observation, yet the real truth of it lies in its implementation."

— *Chris Guillebeau*

Andy and I had exchanged a few emails while he had been out in Fiji. I didn't know him that well at all, but I knew him well enough to wince when he told me that he wanted to do an MBA. That evening, we were at an Escape event that his friend had brought him to. He'd just returned from Fiji, and when I asked him why he wanted to do an MBA, he replied, "I want to start a business. And I think an MBA would give me credibility when I'm raising funding."

"You don't need an MBA," I said to Andy. "Some people need and should do MBAs for legitimate reasons, but when you've got basically zero work experience, you've just gotten back from a long travel stint, and you're telling me you want to do an MBA because you want to start a business…"

I trailed off. I had written a book on the MBA subject and told him about the countless MBA graduates I'd met from some of the best schools in the world, like Harvard and Stanford and London Business School. They had been so book-smart, so driven, and so great at jumping through hoops. They had been the most excellent of the excellent sheep.

But some of them had still been struggling to figure out what it is that they wanted, what they wanted to build. On the other hand, I'd met the owners of successful businesses, who were our age, who had delivered talks at the Escape School.

The more business owners I had heard speak, the more I realised that in the age of the protean career, we all needed to be more entrepreneurial. Even if we didn't plan to run our own businesses someday, it was obvious to me that the resilience, proactivity and determination exemplified by these business owners was something that anyone building a 21st century career needed.

I also met so many people wanting to start their own businesses that I took special note of the advice offered by those who had started businesses in somewhat unique categories. One of these was Gabriella Zavatti, who is the founder of Zavva Concepts Ltd, which produces ZAVVA shots. ZAVVA Shots come in 30ml alcoholic ready-to-drink (RTD) split pot shots and contain two separate but equally complementary flavoured liqueurs.

Being half Australian and half Italian, Gabriella was raised and educated in Hong Kong, the place she calls home. After completing her degree in Australia, Gabriella returned to Hong Kong where she realized there was a demand for a new and innovative RTD beverage.

At the age of 23, Gabriella launched ZAVVA Shots with the goal of developing a homegrown Hong Kong product that represented the characteristics of the city from which it was inspired by, namely an alcoholic beverage that was small, compact, and bursting with energy. Now, ZAVVA shots operates in three markets and continues to expand globally.

Gabby had not realised at the time when she started her business, the extent to which she was not as well equipped or prepared to go down the startup path as most. She had no business background – more than anything she was driven by a huge passion to create and an idea she truly believed could change the way we consume. She said that this made her hungry to build and it gave her the balls to believe she could do so. She graduated from the University of Melbourne with a double major in English Literature and History.

"This didn't teach me the basics of marketing, structuring a business plan, how to make a pitch book, nor did it provide the basis for forming a marketing strategy. What it did teach me, however, was how to be curious," she said, which I told Andy. "I think this is what took me further – to question, to enquire, to delve deeper, to analyse and to evaluate the bigger picture."

"All the other technicalities I learned on-the-go, with a lot of trial and error," she reflects. "It was good to make mistakes early on. I taught myself as I went along; the semantics of logistics, operating a profit and loss statement, negotiation of legal agreements, cohesive branding."

I told Andy that his experiences in Fiji were probably going to help him the way Gabby's international background had helped her.

"I also think that the soft skills I developed through my upbringing, relationships and education facilitated me tremendously," she said. "Having empathy to understand what it is people are communicating, talking to everyone across a diverse range of people you encounter in your day, but really truly genuinely listening."

"You think you need to know everything," I said to Andy. "You don't. You need to do things. That's what people listen to." I reminded him what Gabby had told me about her own journey.

"In hindsight, I actually believe it helped me not having more specialised business education before starting as I learned by doing," she explained. "Just by having an intense interest and passion in what I was doing made me learn faster, and with a lot more street smarts then if I was sitting in a lecture hall taking notes."

"You don't need to achieve everything before you get started," I told Andy. "But you have to actually make a plan to do things, and then do them." Remembering what Gabby had said about her own lack of formal business education, I added that in the LEAN framework, the "achieve" component could be the most relevant to him at this point.

So while Andy resisted the word "achieve", I explained to him that it was actually shorthand for just getting things done – which is what employers (or investors) pay attention to: Results.

"You will never be as knowledgeable or prepared as you would like to be, and often this is used as an excuse not to commence a project or develop an idea," Gabby said. "Once you start, you'll soon realise that with enough focus and perseverance that there is nothing you can't handle or won't solve."

Andy told me that he just wanted someone to give him a load of money so that he could explore his idea. I laughed. "That's not going to happen," I said.

"Well, actually," I paused. "Maybe it could. But what's more likely is that you build something great, and then start speaking to investors *if* investment is what you need."

"You know," I reflected, "A recent speaker at an Escape event said, 'People think businesses raise money in order to become great. It's the other way round… they're great businesses already and that's why they raise money'."

The LEAN framework: Achieve

Andy thought that by 'achieve' I meant that he should become the world's leading expert on the business he wanted to start, which was solar-powered stoves. Instead, what I had been referring to, was gaining traction in an achievable way and doing things that demonstrated your interest in an area. In his case, Andy was trying to potentially raise funding for his idea, but in other cases, I had seen graduates use this approach in landing jobs in organisations that might never have heard of them. In both scenarios, I explained to Andy that the focus of achieving was to do the following:

- **Strengthen your strengths** – You might have a theoretical idea of what your strengths are but until you actually put them into practice, it's all theory. The baseline of fulfilling work is often linked to feeling good about what you do, but many are not sure of what their strengths actually are. The place to begin is usually to start with your interests.

- **Refine your proximate objective** – Many people set out to do something and dream a big dream. Then it gets so big that it overwhelms them and engulfs them and before they know it, they're paralysed. It's so important to start with baby steps. Define the next important thing you have to do, make it realistic and achievable, then go do it.

- **Practice with an audience** – Experiments without an audience are fine, but experiments with an audience are far more powerful. As Sam designed her MVP, it was a yoga session with actual (not theoretical) people, who gave her a different kind of feedback than if she'd been by herself. Similarly, if Andy wanted to figure out what he was good at, it was much more helpful for him if he practiced with actual people involved.

Strengthen Your Strengths

"What are you good at?" I asked Andy.

"I have no idea," he said.

"Well, what would others say you're good at?"

"Beer?" He joked.

I could tell from his stories that Andy had gained a number of skills from his time in Fiji. Perhaps the most obvious one was his ability to approach nearly anyone and to make them feel immediately comfortable with them. He also seemed great at leading a team, which I think he'd learned from his sports team experience at school. I wanted to teach him how to use these strengths to his advantage.

"You need to know what you're good at and what you suck at," I said to Andy. "But you can only find that out through experience. Through setting yourself goals and seeing how you stack up."

"Do you know what kind of business you want to start?" I asked Andy.

"Maybe something with solar-powered stoves," he murmured. "Something they could use in Fiji. I don't know."

I told him that sometimes it was these niche businesses based on personal interests that ended up being incredibly fulfilling. I told him about Robert Welch, who started his own company seven years ago.

Rob founded smallcarBIGCITY – a company that use a fleet of restored classic Mini Coopers to show off the quirky backstreets and hidden gems of London. The company has taken over 25,000 people around since their launch in 2009 and was listed as the No.1 Greatest Thing to do in London by Time Out Magazine in 2012.

Robert is also the CEO of Best London Tours which was founded in 2013 to re-sell the top 1% of attractions and experiences across different mediums of travel. He regularly consults for businesses within the luxury travel and automotive industry. He was the Director of London for Lime & Tonic in 2014 – a digital concierge company for your social life. His latest venture is a classic car brokering firm, launching in the summer of 2016.

"How did he start it?" Andy asked.

I told him that Robert had a 1975 Mini Cooper for his first car. The car came with him to uni in London and he noticed that this elicited a reaction. When he was 23, like many of his peers, he applied for a job at Lehman Brothers and various insurance institutions in September 2008. It was the same week as the financial crash and as a result, there were no jobs in the City.

He knew London very well but was still interested in the city's vast history. He started looking for ways to see the capital that were slightly less touristy than getting on a sightseeing bus. He looked at how much black cabs were charging per hour and wondered if people would be willing to pay a premium to travel in a classic car on a personal trip with a Londoner.

He started taking people out in his car for free, using a 'pay what you think it is worth' tipping culture. As he was earning £80-100 per hour he thought it would make a viable business. So he

founded smallcarBIGITY in December 2008. He needed £30,000 to launch the business.

Banks were not interested so he needed private investment. He met Oliver Knight and Alastair Bruton – they all put in the cash, bought two more cars, got the relevant licences and insurances and started trading in August 2009.

They now have 8 cars and 17 drivers, have taken 25,000 happy customers around, were listed the No. 1 Best Thing To Do In London in June 2012, have been awarded the Certificate of Excellence on TripAdvisor for the last 6 years in a row and work with brands such as Aston Martin, Google, Facebook and Firefox.

When I had asked Rob about his hesitations on starting the business, he told me the following, which I relayed back to Andy.

"The biggest hesitation I had before starting was over that internal fear of failure – of letting those closest to me down," Rob said. "And not being able to provide for my family, being humiliated and being forced into a 'normal' job that I was not passionate about."

On the MBA point, I told Andy that Rob had said, "Personally I feel the rate at which you learn and adapt on the job is far greater than reading about a theoretical process."

"I think the values that you are brought up with are far more important than the education," Rob remarked. "If you have decent values and principles in place, education should be something that is self-taught as much as conscripted through academia."

Andy nodded. "Where do I start, then?"

"I think you start with your strengths," I told him. "You're great at approaching people, and bringing people together. Approach some people about your idea who know more than you do about solar-powered stoves. Interview them, see what they say. Take them out for coffee."

"You're a good talker," I said to him. "And if you love Fiji, and the people there, and solar power, and stoves, I have no doubt you could do *something* in this space."

As Rob had said, which I passed onto Andy: "Fundamentally, if you are passionate and driven in what you are doing, you will produce something of value that people are willing to invest in. I strongly believe that success is a by-product of doing what you love and doing it really well."

Refine Your Proximate Objective

Andy took the advice and spent the next week sending off emails here and there. He emailed me a couple of weeks later and told me that while he'd had some replies, he still had no idea where to go next. What was his grand plan? Or should he focus on small steps?

I told him that the best approach was probably somewhere in the middle – using small steps to build up a grand plan. I told him about *Good Strategy/Bad Strategy,* written by Richard Rumelt.

The book talks about how rare good strategy is. While Rumelt talks about this in the context of organisations, it can still apply to career development.

Good strategy, Rumelt says, is not the same as having a set of performance goals, or worse, a set of vague aspirations. "Bad strategy" happens when there is bad doctrine, difficult choices are avoided, or leaders are unwilling to define and explain the nature of the challenge.

Rumelt also talks about how one of a leader's most powerful tools is the creation of a proximate objective—one that is close enough at hand to be feasible. A proximate objective names an accomplishment that an organisation can reasonably be expected to achieve.

Since "proximate objective" is quite a mouthful, I prefer to call them "small steps" or "baby steps".

I saw this in practice when Matt Robinson, one of the founders of GoCardless, came in to speak at an Escape event.

GoCardless is now one of Europe's leading recurring payment providers having collected over $1 billion for companies like The Guardian, The FT and Box.com and has raised more than $25 million from some of the world's leading investors including Accel Partners, Balderton Capital, Passion Capital and Y Combinator.

Robinson is a former McKinsey & Company consultant and Oxford Law student. He and his McKinsey colleague Hiroki Takeuchi founded GoCardless after leaving their jobs in the City, along with Tom Blomfield. They went through Paul Graham's famed Y Combinator accelerator program.

Matt had just launched a new company, Nested.com, in the property space. Reflecting on what he had learned so far as an entrepreneur, Matt told the Escape audience that the key to getting started was "supreme focus".

"At the start, there are only two things you need to worry about, and nothing else," Matt said. "Firstly, building your product; and secondly, talking to your users. If you haven't got any users, talk to the people who you think might be your users."

I had seen Andy run around thinking about marketing and which website program he should use to launch his website. But

I passed on Matt's advice: "Legal, accounts, all the other bullshit – chuck it out of the window. What really matters is asking yourself, 'Will we be alive in 12 months time?'"

"When and how do you approach investors?" Andy wondered.

When it comes to finding investment, Matt had said, "All you need is a graph that shows growth. If you haven't got that, the reality is you probably shouldn't be worrying about investment anyway. The metrics to focus on are ideally revenue, or significant user growth – or the equivalent in your industry."

Matt also pointed out, "You're on this planet for a really short space of time, and if you get the investment, you're committed to this for at least 12-18 months. So I want and need to be *more* convinced than the investors that this is something I should be spending 12-18 months of my life on."

I pointed out to Andy that right now, he needed to set himself a proximate objective that was realistic and *achievable*. So he committed to building a two-page business plan of his assumptions based on the conversations he was having with people in the space, and if it made sense, building a prototype of the solar-powered stove within the next six months. He said it depended on whether he could find prospective customers.

"At least you have something to aim for now," I said. "A proximate objective."

"That's just a fancy word for 'baby step'," Andy replied.

PRACTICE WITH AN AUDIENCE

Once Andy had decided his next steps, we started talking about what would happen if he did in fact get his prototype together.

"I think it's important not to develop things in isolation," I said to him. "Involving people in your journey as early as possible means that you not only getting early customer feedback but that you also get important advice and input as you're still developing what you're building."

"It's so tempting to wait until something's perfect before you 'launch' it," I told him. But some of the best businesses I've seen, especially the interesting and unique ones, have been developed in front of an audience the whole time.

I told Andy about Jenny Costa (née Dawson), the founder of Rubies in the Rubble, a social business that concocts luxury preserves out of food destined for the garbage as a way of raising awareness about food waste globally. She worked at a hedge fund before quitting her job.

One morning, she set her alarm for 4am and cycled down to the hub of London's fruit and vegetable trading, New Covent Garden Market at Nine Elms. She was horrified to find, just a few feet away from the market traders, skip after skip of food destined for the scrapheap, including mangoes from the Philippines and tomatoes from Turkey. While perfectly edible, they simply hadn't been sold. Some were misshapen, so would be rejected by supermarkets, but a lot was simply surplus.

She was struck by the lack of morality in the situation where food is brought in from Africa, low prices are demanded, and there remains such glut when it arrives that it can then be thrown away.

Jenny began researching food waste and found that we throw out 7.2 million tonnes of food in the UK every year. The financial price tag is £12 billion a year – but the cost to the environment is enormous, too.

A week later, Jenny was back at the market and filled the basket of her bike and the rucksack with as many tomatoes, onions and apples as she could. She also rang her Mum for her chutney recipe. She began boiling up batches of chutney on the stove with a friend, and she took a market stall in Marylebone High Street to sell the early version of her products.

Their spicy chutney completely sold out, earning them £200. Afterwards they went for a pub lunch to warm up, and she realised, "This is what I want to do."

Jenny began selling her chutneys at Borough Market, and is now stocked at Selfridges, Fortnum & Mason, independent delis, and Waitrose.

Jenny had not only set herself small steps, but she had gone out and launched an early version of her idea at the markets.

"She'd gotten real feedback, from real people, and real inspiration," I told Andy. "You can't just lock yourself away and then unleash your grand idea on the world after you've already developed it."

"You need to practice with an audience," I told him. "If you're going to do any kind of product, this means getting it in front of people as often as possible, taking the prototype to meetings with you, speaking at events if you can, starting a meetup."

"If you're going to do teaching," I said to him, remembering Sam's story, "This means practicing with actual students."

"I get it," Andy said. "I'm a little shy when it comes to that stuff but I see the value in actually having customers in the room as you develop what you're building."

SUMMARY

"So, what have we learned, Andy?" I joked.

He grinned. "Get stronger what I'm strong at. Set baby steps, or baby goals, and hit them. Practice with an audience."

"And what does this mean for the coming month?"

He paused. "I need to start approaching people – putting my 'good talker' skills to use including manufacturers and designers. I actually need to look at my diary to figure out how much time I have and what goals I can realistically set. And I'll make sure to keep developing this with the prospective audience as much as possible."

I held up my hand for a high five, which he slapped.

"Boom," I said.

[7]

NETWORK

"Opportunities do not float like clouds in the sky. They're attached to people. If you're looking for an opportunity, you're really looking for a person."

— *Ben Casnocha*

Nadia was at a nightclub with some friends and felt like everyone else around her was having fun, but that no matter what she did, she felt alone and lost and grey. What was wrong with her? The ice rattled in her vodka Sprite as she gave it a shake and tried to focus on the conversation around her.

It was about some comment that some guy had said to some girl and then she'd said something back about someone else and… she lost track. Plus she couldn't really hear over the techno remix, which was a sign that the night was winding down.

She didn't remember the details of where she was or why they were there. What she remembered very clearly was being intensely bored and hating that feeling.

Her public self was having fun: great friends, interesting classes, pretty involved in campus life. Her private self was in hell. Underneath these moments, there was a grey sense of dread; a secret psychological tumour that grew the closer she got to graduation.

She would forget about the greyness when caught in a great conversation or laughing with someone, or staring into the eyes of a close friend or cute guy or kissing someone or learning someone's secrets or telling them hers: the world would feel open and life would feel as though it made sense. Then it would pass.

It was this loop playing incessantly at the root of her consciousness. No matter how much yoga she did or how much she drank or shopped, when the hangover hit or the lights came back on, she was left with the sneaking suspicion that she was missing something, as if each day was the tail-end of a conversation that she should have been paying more attention to.

She hated being stuck on this treadmill, forced by her own hand into investing in a hologram of herself, a conglomeration of what her parents wanted her to do, what her friends thought she would do, what her peers were going to do, but excluding what she wanted to do, or who she wanted to become. She felt like she was losing her ability to read herself, and it felt like shit.

The further into the semester she had gotten, the harder it had become to ignore the shrinking runway separating her campus life from that zone beyond the visible horizon. As long as she tried to ignore that vacuum, she was fine. Then there would be times when she'd fall into a spiral of, *I have no idea what I want to do with my life, I'm graduating soon, I'm going to have to decide or someone else will decide for me, but I have no idea how I should even decide, where do I go, what do I do…*

When a friend of her older sister had mentioned a last-minute opening for an unpaid internship with her department, Nadia accepted in an instant. The trouble was, she had borrowed money from her parents in order to be able to move to London, and she had absolutely no idea how she was ever going to pay them back if this failed to turn into a paid position.

Sometimes she was grateful for the internship. Other times she remembered that it wasn't a "real" job. She worried that if she left the internship, nothing better would come along, and then she'd be even worse off than where she started. She felt completely clueless as to what her "passion" was and felt like she couldn't make a move until she figured it out.

Nadia's sister was a friend of mine and sent Nadia to have a coffee with me. When I met Nadia, I told her about the PERMA Model, which was developed by respected positive psychologist, Martin Seligman (the same psychologist who came up with the Learned Optimism explanatory style, which we explored earlier).

PERMA is a framework for measuring well-being, I explained to Nadia. The acronym stands for the five essential elements ideally in place to encourage lasting well-being: Positive emotion, Engagement, Relationships, Meaning and purpose, and Accomplishment. No single element defines well-being, but each contributes to it.

"If you're feeling low on the 'meaning' scale," I said to Nadia. "Maybe it comes from feeling disconnected from the people around you."

She nodded but didn't say anything, so I barged on.

"It's worth remembering that your career is going to be determined by the people you meet," I said to her. "Whether it's the person interviewing you for a new role, or someone who introduces you to a company – we often get preoccupied figuring out what we should know or who we should know but really, it's more about who knows us."

The LEAN framework: Network

I explained to Nadia some of the trends I had noticed not only from being hired but also from doing the hiring myself.

"When you think of the company hiring you," I said to Nadia. "Think of yourself as an asset. You have skills, knowledge, contacts and experience. Your goal is to maximise yourself as an asset, to make yourself as valuable as possible to a prospective company."

I told Nadia how in the early days of yMedia, we had emailed Rod Drury, the CEO of accounting software business Xero. The email had been ignored – rightfully so – as at that point in time we hadn't necessarily done or proven anything. After yMedia started to gain traction, and we spoke at a national conference where Rod Drury was in the audience, he approached us and eventually became a mentor of mine.

"If you're aiming to be mentored by people who are amazing, you have to try to be as amazing as possible yourself," I said to her. "Amazing at what you do, producing amazing results, and so on."

"How?" She asked. I outlined the following.

- **Connect through contribution** – Networking is painful and it can be really awkward to stand in a room full of strangers handing out your business card. So instead, reframe networking in your mind as a way of connecting with those in your industry so that you are better placed to contribute significantly to your chosen sector in the long run.

- **Approach mentors intelligently** – The people you want to have as mentors will often be far too busy to even respond to your emails. So it's important to approach them with specific asks, that do not weigh on their time, and can directly help them. It's even better to build up credibility and confidence in yourself by focusing on your own career wins and getting as much positive traction as possible before you approach them.

- **Create your own hub** – Having peers who have similar goals to you can be incredibly beneficial at any stage in your career. Even people who have been working for 20 years tend to have groups they regularly meet with, of peers in similar positions in their industry. Some people call these "mastermind groups" but I think regardless of what the label is, it's important to be regularly meeting with others who hold you accountable to your goals.

CONNECT THROUGH CONTRIBUTION

When I was explaining to Nadia how to reframe herself as a contributor, I told her that essentially it came down to being a great team player. I shared the common characteristics I had noticed from the strongest people I had worked with over the years. They could each be defined as great team players.

Commitment. A great team player is someone you can rely on, even when (*especially* when) things are tough. You want them to do what they say they're going to do, meet deadlines, and provide a consistent stream of high-quality work. Doers beat talkers, every day.

Confident, constructive communication. Great team players speak about their ideas honestly and clearly and respect the views and opinions of others on the team. They share their thoughts and ideas clearly, directly, honestly, and they're considerate too.

Flexible and positive. Great team players don't get rattled or complain but are flexible and can deal with whatever is thrown their way. Taking on more responsibilities and extra initiative sets them apart.

Proactive. Great team players don't passively wait for things to happen; they make things happen. They show up prepared for team meetings and listen and speak up in discussions. They take the initiative to help make things happen, and they put their hand up for assignments. Their driving belief is can-do: "What contribution can I make to help the team achieve success?"

Solution-focused. Great team players are problem-solvers. Instead of dwelling on, allocating blame, or avoiding a problem, they acknowledge and deal with executing a solution. They don't simply talk about the problem, look for others to fault, or put off dealing with issues. They just get on with making the solution into a reality.

I also explained to Nadia that besides the above, an underlying trait for great team players tends to be that they have growth mindsets as opposed to fixed mindsets.

This is something I learned when I interviewed Dr Tara Swart, CEO of the Unlimited Mind, Faculty at MIT Sloan and lead author of the book *Neuroscience for Leadership: Harnessing the Brain Gain Advantage*. She referenced Dr Carol Dweck's work on fixed mindsets and growth mindsets.

The Fixed Mindset: According to Dweck, a Type 1 or fixed mindset is one that is fearful of making mistakes. With this mindset, you're excellent at playing by the rules, great at behaving yourself and a consistent achiever when it comes to good grades, which have led to good degrees and good jobs. You've been indoctrinated to believe that the fixed mindset is the route to success.

"To fail is shame inducing and painful, as the right ventro-lateral pre-frontal cortex is firing off all sorts of pain signals and the cortisol levels are rising," Dr. Swart explains. "Shame is one of the five basic human emotions that fall into the "avoidance" category – you will do anything not to feel like this."

The Growth Mindset: Dr Swart explains that Type 2 or Growth mindsets fear losing out on opportunities: "Type 2 mindset people would feel ashamed if they sat on the side lines whilst someone else ran off with a great idea. The way they work, gold nuggets emerge as 'aha' moments of insight that guide towards step changes in innovation."

For a person with a growth mindset, "failure is not bad and it can even be exciting."

To develop an innovative mindset, she talks about the importance of learning to combine "empathy for the context of a problem, creativity in the generation of insights and solutions and rationality to analyse and fit solutions to the context."

Improving the art of combining empathy, creativity, and rationality seems to be a skill that can only be honed through multiple experiments and failures.

The growth mindset is encouraged, Dr Swart says, by "re-igniting that curious childhood spirit that can get squelched by formal education and corporate life."

How can you encourage a growth mindset and get rid of a fixed mindset? By channelling advice from Marc Eckō, an American fashion designer and entrepreneur who turned a $5,000 investment into a billion dollar fashion and lifestyle company might be a good place to start. He said in an INC article:

"I can tell you... that success doesn't look like an 'A+'. And failure isn't as simple as an 'F'. Failure could be very grey. You might arrive at an event in your life where you think, 'Wow I've succeeded,' and be getting the affirmation from all these outside forces, but if it's not aligned authentically to who you are, it can very much feel like failure," he says.

He rebrands the art of making mistakes with his observation that "success is merely the hangover of failure."

"I think we're taught in the system that failure is something that you should be ashamed of. Failure is for the dumb kids. You get an 'F'. You get a 'D'. You didn't comply. You didn't create the evidence of your worthiness," he says.

Failure, he argues, is a crucial element in building a unique learning atmosphere for yourself: more failures lead to more lessons that lead to more success.

I told Nadia that if she was aiming to be a great team player, and adopted a growth mindset, she would already outpace most of the graduates I met who were looking for a job.

"I'm scared of getting things wrong, I guess," she admitted, when we talked about the fixed vs. growth mindset.

"Look, I know you don't necessarily want to start your own business," I told her. "But I think you'd enjoy this story about Charlie Thuillier, who left Diageo to start Oppo ice cream."

After almost a year of working his graduate job at Diageo, at 23 years old, Charlie left in order to found Oppo. He pitched up on his brother's Harry's sofa which became Charlie's home for the next nine months and then sofa-surfed around friends' flats for a further four months. In December 2012 Charlie approached seven brand agencies without a product.

"It was a chicken-and-egg situation where I needed the branding to be able to convince the factory; the factory to create the product; the product to get the branding, yet no money to get any" he said. Still, he managed to convince one of the UK's top agencies to brand Oppo, a British factory to help create the product, and both to work for no charge.

Launched in October 2014, Oppo is now in 1,300 locations around the UK including Wholefoods Market, Co-Op, Budgens, Holland & Barrett, as well as sports clubs, offices, hospitals, cinemas and hotels. Oppo has been awarded the Guardian's Start up of the Year, won the Healthy Food Guide Award, and accompanied the PM David Cameron on the Queen's jet to Milan to showcase the best of British innovation.

"But you know how they got there?" I said to Nadia, "It took *25 months* of research, *three* different factories, two specialised food research centres, and four grants from Santander, York University and the British government to fully launch."

I told her, "Do you think if Charlie had a fixed mindset, that it would have gotten off the ground? No way!"

"Charlie, in my opinion," I shared with her, "Is an enormously positive person. He saw opportunities where others saw challenges – this is an example of the growth mindset in action."

"Connecting through contribution means pegging yourself to something larger than yourself," I said to Nadia. "Right now, that might mean making yourself as invaluable as possible to your current team. But also find ways that you can talk to or work with other teams in the organisation. Focus on being a great team player, creating opportunities for yourself, and don't get put off by setbacks."

"What happened to Oppo?" Nadia asked.

"After launching into 117 Waitrose stores and on Ocado.com in October 2014, they also launched and closed a second round of crowdfunding on Seedrs in 2015, reaching £150,000 in just six hours (for 5% of the business), and overfunding to £353,811 with over 550 investors."

"Wow," she said.

"Whether you're working for someone else or running your own business," I said to her. "The principle is the same – it's not about you. It's about making the team you're on, stronger. Making the organisation you're working for, stronger."

APPROACH MENTORS INTELLIGENTLY

Nadia wanted to get to know some of the senior editors at her magazine but wasn't sure how to approach them. I told her to remember that they're insanely busy people, so to keep any email contact short, concise, and focused on them instead of on her.

"You also need to know what you're asking for," I said to her. "Make it difficult for them to refuse, and very easy for them to say yes to a specific ask. If you can be very specific about what you can do for them, they're likely to say yes."

"And don't forget basic manners," I added. "Do what you said you would, be punctual, be grateful, be genuine. Thank them for letting you help them."

Another approach, I told her, was to remember that the better you get at what you're doing, the less difficult it becomes to approach people who might have once seemed out of reach. I used Jade Gross as an example.

About six years ago, Jade was about to finish her Master's in International Development at the London School of Economics and told me that she was thinking of applying to law school.

As someone who had dropped out of law school only a matter of months ago, I felt well-placed to tell her that it might not be what she thought it was going to be. She had come around to my place and was sitting on my couch. When I heard her news, I paced over to my bookshelf, pulled my Torts textbook off the shelf, and handed it to her. It was so painfully brand-new that it cracked as I opened it.

"That is law school," I said.

Jade mentioned that she'd also been checking out culinary schools. If she applied, would I write her a reference? Of course I agreed. She ended up applying to a culinary school in Paris, called Ecole Grégoire-Ferrandi, and she got in.

Now, if she had written to any prospective mentors at this point – any big chefs she wanted to meet – who knows if they would have responded to her email? What did she have to contribute at this point? Still, she focused on being a great team player, even when things were challenging.

"When I was in culinary school, it was hard to adapt to the new scenery, the new environment and a different way of thinking, some people I studied with, already had some sort of culinary background, compared to me who used to make dinner at home and cook for myself and friends sometimes," she says.

During her studies, she had to pick a place to intern in. "I wanted the hardest and I wanted the best. I think it was not only to prove to others but to prove to myself, to push myself to the limit and see how far I can last, how far I can grow, how much I can learn?"

Jade worked in Alain Ducasse at the Plaza Athénée hotel, a 3-Michelin star restaurant in the heart of Paris.

"I cried many times, I was the only girl in that restaurant and life in the kitchen is also about dealing with a lot of bullshit that happens in it." But she dealt with it. And when she finished, she went to travel in Brazil and did a little stint at D.O.M, now a 2-star Michelin in Sao Paolo. Then she applied to many restaurants, one of them being Mugaritz, still a 2-Star Michelin restaurant on the outskirts of San Sebastian.

These days, Jade can approach pretty much anyone she wants in the culinary industry. As she reflects:

"I realise I had 'made it', when I was offered the position of Chef de Cuisine (head chef) of the restaurant last year. They asked me? They considered me? You must be joking. That is something I felt was so unimaginable and hard to reach, yet four years in the industry, and three of them in Mugaritz, helped me propel to that position. I think I felt even more of a high when they asked me to join the Research and Development team, where the turnover is very, very, very low."

"So what you're saying," Nadia said, "Is that I need to focus on what I can control, which is producing amazing work and outcomes, and that as I get better at what I do, I'll be able to approach more mentors."

"Yes," I said. "You should also hear about the struggles Jade went through, as I think you might find them relevant."

I told her that Jade came from a family where one of her parents is Asian and a little more conservative. As her dissatisfaction with her master's grew, so too did her passion for cooking.

"I tried to seek something that would make me happy inside no matter the cost," Jade says of her career change. "With this, comes fear, fear of disappointment, fear of failing, fear of it just being a hobby and not more. Am I really willing to take a risk and change everything at the age of 23? Should I just stay on the path and be more secure? Will I rise after I fall? How will my friends see me? How will my peers see me? How far will I go in this industry, will I succeed at all?"

I told Nadia that sometimes, we cannot produce amazing work until we have a little more faith in ourselves to be capable of doing so. I shared what Jade had told me about her own early days.

"My confidence was definitely not as high as it is now," Jade says. "Passion came first and without passion, it is harder to build up competence. But as I continued to put one foot in front of another, and took each step as it came, doing my best each time... new opportunities opened up for me."

CREATE YOUR OWN HUB

"Right now," Nadia said. "I don't feel ready to approach any mentors. I'd rather meet more like-minded peers, actually."

"Totally," I said to her. "I think that sometimes that can be even more valuable."

I told Nadia that when it comes to making pivotal decisions, it's tempting to try and predict beyond what we can actually know. However, it's impossible to know what our future self is going to want, or what the "right" opportunity might look like for our future self.

Instead, it seems like a smarter bet to create nooks within an environment where we can be interested, engaged, and of service to those around us. Sometimes this can mean finding our heroes or idols and continuing on their work with them or for them.

Creating your own hub, I explained to Nadia, is like playing a new sport and making a plan to regularly kick the ball around with players from another team.

"It's as simple as thinking of two or three people you feel are on your wavelength and want the same things," I said to Nadia. "And approaching them about meeting up for coffee every two weeks, and setting goals in the meantime."

I told her about two arrangements where I still had this – I meet up with a writing friend fortnightly to make sure we were both on track with goals we'd set ourselves, and I meet up with two female entrepreneurs each month to reflect and plan on the bigger picture of what we're working on, which can sometimes be easy to lose in the day-to-day.

While we usually have a loose agenda (each person goes through their progress over the past timeframe, the problems and plans they're anticipating for the next little while), the conversation often turns to broader strategic issues that we're facing.

"So it's as simple as just setting up a recurring calendar invite, and finding the right people to meet up with," I said to her. "Sometimes it doesn't work out or life gets in the way, but if it's a fit, you'll make it work."

"At this stage in life, in your twenties, you're still an apprentice in anything you do." I said to Nadia, "The important thing is to find your wizards, the masters in your field. Sometimes they're in industry, sometimes they're in academia." These are the people whose wisdom and knowledge you want to absorb, I said; whose paths you want to partly emulate.

To be able to recognise your wizards, you need to first figure out what your deepest values are, what you're trying to learn more about – what excites and interests you, what you could read about all day long, what you could spend your whole life exploring and contributing towards. While those answers are not for sale, they seem to be the ones we end up spending the most on trying to find.

Sometimes your wizards end up being your business partners. I told Nadia the story of how the founders behind Escape the City decided to start their own journey.

* * *

"The corporate treadmill is, "You send it to me, I'll redraft it, you draft it back, I'll draft it back to you, then we'll send it up for sign-off," Rob explained to me, when he was telling me the story of how Escape the City started.

In 2009, Rob had been working at Ernst & Young in London: "For the first time in my life, I completely lost my devotion – a straight-A student, never dropped the ball – and there I was, slacking my way through my weeks. I was like; 'I'm 25. If I wait another year, I'll be 26. What will I have gained here? Another 20,000 pounds saved, maybe? 15,000 pounds?' Time is fucking short – I'm just not prepared to do it."

While you'd have to be at work about 10 hours a day, only three of those would be productive hours. "It's amazing how you can get away with that and everyone thinks you're doing a great job and you feel like an absolute sham. It's not because you're slacking, it's just because the system is structured in the way that you will be sitting around waiting for someone to sign off a PowerPoint deck until 8:00 at night – when you'd actually start working at 4, and you're like, 'This is such a waste of my time and their time – everyone's time.'"

If we are what we repeatedly do, the feeling of worthlessness that I often saw becomes easier to explain. If we're constantly wasting time, without pleasure or direction or purpose, perhaps we ourselves begin to feel like a walking waste of time.

A job at a big company, says entrepreneur and investor Paul Graham, can be like high fructose corn syrup: "It has some of the qualities of things you're meant to like, but is disastrously lacking in others." He points out that humans have not been designed to ingest white flour, refined sugar, high fructose corn syrup, and hydrogenated vegetable oil, yet these four ingredients account for most of the calories in your typical grocery store.

"If people have to choose between something that's cheap, heavily marketed, and appealing in the short term, and something that's expensive, obscure, and appealing in the long term, which do you think most will choose?" He links that philosophy to work: working in a big company seems much more "normal" – so the average graduate from a top university will probably want to land a corporate gig, "because it's a recognised brand, it's safe, and they'll get paid a good salary right away."

Yet this environment seems a false construct for the way humans are meant to spend 75 percent of their year and 75 percent of their life. As Graham describes, "It's the job equivalent of the pizza they had for lunch. The drawbacks will only become apparent later, and then only in a vague sense of malaise." The onset of that malaise is the point at which they join Escape the City and their name lands on our database. This malaise is exactly what the co-founders, Rob and Dom, were feeling at Ernst & Young in London, back in 2009, when they started to develop the idea that would set them free.

Rob told me that they would meet up on Friday for lunch, and talk about what they would be doing if not this. One week, Dom showed Rob this web site called FleetheCity.co.uk, which was a charity site that he built to fundraise for a Yukon canoe race that he was doing that summer of 2009. Dom was spending all his money and holiday time doing crazy adventures, so that "at least for some portion of the year I'd feel alive." He said to Rob, "I think there's an opportunity to build a web site for corporate people who want to spend their money on crazy adventures – the Yukon race, Marathon des Sables in the Sahara, that kind of thing."

Dom had always read entrepreneurial books and been interested in startups. Rob thought it was a cool idea, but at that stage, Rob recalls, "He wasn't offering me to work with him on it – he wasn't even seriously going to work on it. There was just this little kernel of an idea." The moment when they resigned would only come later, but for now, they'd go to lunch on Fridays – "somewhere far enough away from the building so that people wouldn't hear us plotting." Rob began subscribing to blogs and would keep a black moleskin filled with scribbles. "I subscribed to the McKinsey Quarterly and I was using all my logins to access all the knowledge databases – but guess what I was researching? Exciting business stuff, not how British Telecom can cut the costs of head count."

* * *

When talking about his own resignation, Rob refers to that Steve Jobs quote: "For the past 33 years, I have looked in the mirror every morning and asked myself: 'If today were the last day of my life, would I want to do what I am about to do today?' And whenever the answer has been 'No' for too many days in a row, I know I need to change something." The trigger came one Friday, when he sat at his cubicle and watched another round-robin email from "the Banter Bus" pop up in his email inbox.

"Some old school friends of mine – one worked at a bank, one worked at a law firm – they'll email each other like a hundred times a day with in-jokes, and talking about football, girls and sometimes, one person will have an extra long amount of time that they don't have to work. They'll put together an email which is images instead of words – "Eye" "fucking" – and that would be an image of someone having sex – "hate" "this job" and all this stuff and they put it together."

"So I remember one of these was going around on a Friday and I was like, 'Oh, I just gotta get out of here. I just want to escape.' So I googled the word "escape" and then hit "Images" and the first thing that comes up is this little photo of an escape key walking. 'That's quite cool,' I thought, I just sent it to Dom – without any words. I got what can only be described as this flood of enthusiasm back on an email and him going, "Yes! That's it! It's not flee, it's escape!" I was like, "What's he talking about? Oh yeah – he must still be talking about the adventure thing." I didn't think much more of it, and then at some point that weekend, he sent me an image, which was the first iteration of the logo for Escthecity.com, and he'd bought the domain, and he was like, 'This is it.'"

The perfect resignation opportunity surfaced when it came to Rob's annual "really awful assessment thing where you ask everyone to review you" – a process he describes as similar to student politics, where you have to canvas for votes, going around to your senior colleagues asking for feedback. This round robin feedback gives you a grade out of 5, but there are quotas, so everyone has to fit into each one of the categories – if you're in the bottom quotas, you're on your way out. Rob explained, "If you hadn't pissed anyone off and all the rest of it, you were going to get a good grade." When people talk about wanting to escape "office politics", I imagine that this is what they're talking about: the process is driven by relationships, rather than pure performance.

This time, he just "didn't have the energy to fake the whole 'will you give me some feedback' thing." Since the process takes about 15 or 20 hours to complete, he decided that he'd either have to explain to his careers counsellor at Ernst & Young why he hadn't completed the exercise, or he'd have to "just man up and quit." Around that time, Dom had also gone to the Yukon for two weeks to do the canoe race, and he'd left Rob with a fateful parting remark.

Rob admits, "If anyone ever challenges me on anything and says, 'You'll never do it,' I always do it... be it shave my head, buy a double-decker bus, drive through Africa or resign. It's like *Back to the Future* where he goes, 'Don't call me chicken!' Dom's like, 'Bet you're not going to be resigned by the time I get back,' and I was like, 'Oh God. What did you do?'"

As it turns out, Rob did resign while Dom was away. As he describes in *The Escape Manifesto*, they felt like they were being carried along by an invisible force. A force with its own agenda, values, and definitions of success – "The Travelator." He defined it as "the conventional path that most graduates and professionals find themselves on." As he explains, the Travelator infers a level of conformity and passivity. "Stepping off The Travelator is hard. It's hard enough to notice that you are even on it."

SUMMARY

The reason why the Escape story is important, I said to Nadia, is because Rob and Dom created a hub between the two of them without even realising it. They were colleagues and shared the same frustrations. They started meeting up without necessarily knowing where it was going to lead. They were simply interested in the same things.

Through that process, they created Escape the City, which eventually led to me working with them. And that, I told Nadia, led to us having coffee now.

"It's a beautiful example of connecting through contribution," I said to Nadia. "These two guys just wanted to help others who were feeling the same pain they were at the time."

Nadia said, "So I need to focus on connecting through contributing, which at the moment for me means being a great team player. I'll approach those senior editors when I'm a bit clearer on what I could offer them, in the form of a specific ask. And I'll email a couple of others I know who are chasing similar dreams, and make a plan to meet up with them regularly."

I didn't know how to tell Nadia that so much of all of this depended on luck. I wasn't about to get into a philosophical debate with her on the extent to which we create our own luck, but I had shared with her the story of Rob and Dom to demonstrate a concept that was hard to articulate.

The only way I could describe it is that we can work hard and try to meet as many people as we can, but as New York Times columnist Frank Bruni put it, "We meet the places we wind up loving much the way we meet the people we fall for: on purpose and accidentally; at precisely the right moment and exactly the wrong time; in the highest of spirits and the lowest of moods."

[8]

GOING LEAN

"Human life occurs only once, and the reason we cannot determine which of our decisions are good and which bad is that in a given situation we can make only one decision; we are not granted a second, third or fourth life in which to compare various decisions."

— *Milan Kundera*

There were islands of cameras that day; everywhere I looked, there seemed to be a smiling graduate in a gown with their parents. I weaved my way through the chatter and laughter and hugs, the questions and introductions – "These are my parents; this is my friend Nick," – "Can you take a photo of me with my Mum?" – "When do you take off for the break?" In only a few hours, hundreds of flashes captured thousands of pictures.

Nadia, Charlie, Andy and Sam all experienced similar graduation ceremonies. So did countless graduates all across the world. As we've seen from this book, the four of them had varying experiences. What they all had in common is that they believed in what Amazon founder Jeff Bezos called "the Regret Minimization Framework".

When Bezos was thinking about quitting his high-paying hedge fund job on Wall Street to start a website called amazon.com, he decided that he wanted to "minimize the number of regrets" he'd have, and called this his Regret Minimization Framework. He said:

"I knew that when I was 80 I was not going to regret having tried this. I was not going to regret trying to participate in this thing called the Internet that I thought was going to be a really big deal. And I knew that if I failed, I wouldn't regret that. But I knew the one thing I might regret is not ever having tried. And I knew that that would haunt me everyday. So when I thought about it that way, it was an incredibly easy decision."

It is so easy to think of all the terrible things that might happen if we venture out of our comfort zone. The scarier thing is wondering what happens if we *don't* do so. The only reason your comfort zone is the size it is, is because you've designed it that way by remaining there. As simple as it sounds, if you feel braver, you simply need to do things that make you uncomfortable. Then, by definition, your comfort zone grows. This philosophy is one that was followed by the LEAN graduates mentioned in this book, who are all still in early stages of their careers.

Charlie started creating a more targeted CV to various small companies he was interested in and took on a junior management role at a tech startup. Nadia's internship turned into a full-time paid position at the magazine. Sam ended up leaving her management consulting role and now does a mixture of dance education, freelance consulting, and creative writing. Andy decided not to pursue the solar-powered ovens idea and instead joined an education charity.

I strongly believe in all the concepts that I have mentioned throughout the framework. The challenges we face in navigating 21st century work environments are opportunities to reset unhelpful scripts from the past, whether they are collective or individual in nature. I hope that this book helps to illustrate that no matter where you are in your career, it is never too late to take steps in a new direction.

ACKNOWLEDGMENTS

To Pamela Minett, for the amazing adventure that preceded all others. Thanks also to Stephen Tindall for providing us with initial funding and to Eddy Helm and Jade Tang for growing yMedia into what it eventually became.

I'm grateful to the contributors who were generous enough to share their journeys, and to the graduates who were kind enough to share their stories with me.

Thanks to Kate Lewington, Mark Jones and Mark Hosking for their editing help in the early stages; to Nikesh Akar for his help with the initial website design for Outbound Book, and to We Make Websites for the Shopify site.

Special thanks to Kat McDonald for her excellent editing skills and to Ivan Cruz and Catherine Chi for their design skills.

Thanks to my family and friends for their constant support and love; special thanks to Rob, Dom and Mikey for starting the Escape family (without which I might never have discovered the material contained in this book).

REFERENCES

Avent, Ryan. "Why Do We Work So Hard?" The Economist 1843 April/May 2016. Web. 20 May. 2016.

https://www.1843magazine.com/features/why-do-we-work-so-hard

Bauman, Zygmont. *Liquid Modernity.* Blackwell Publishers, 2000. Print.

Baxter, Sarah. "The Odyssey Generation Just Won't Grow Up". The Sunday Times Oct. 2007. Web. 20 May. 2016

http://www.thesundaytimes.co.uk/sto/news/world_news/article73469.ece

Brooks, David. "It's Not About You" The New York Times May. 2011. Web. 21 May 2016. http://www.nytimes.com/2011/05/31/opinion/31brooks.html?_r=0

Brown, Philip, Lauder, Hugh and Ashton, David. *The Global Auction.* Oxford University Press Inc, 2011. Print.

Csikszentmihalyi, Mihaly. *Flow: The Psychology of Optimal Experience.* Harper Perennial Modern Classics, 2008. Print.

Deresiewicz, William. *Excellent Sheep: The Miseducation of the American Elite and the Way to a Meaningful Life.* Free Press, 2015. Print.

Deresiewicz, William. "The Disadvantages of an Elite Education." The American Scholar, Jun. 2008. Web. 20 May. 2016. https://theamericanscholar.org/the-disadvantages-of-an-elite education/#.Vz9NZSMrIb0

Dweck, Carol. *Mindset: The New Psychology of Success.* Ballantine Books, 2007. Print.

Escape the City. "What Unites People Who Do Work They Love?" Jan 22 2015. Web. 20 May. 2016 http://blog.escapethecity. org/2015/01/22/unites-people-work-love/

Escape the City. *The Escape Manifesto: Quit Your Corporate Job – Do Something Different!* Capstone, 2013. Print.

Marantz Henig, Robin. "What Is It About 20-Somethings?" The New York Times, 18 Aug 2010. Web. 20 May. 2016

http://www.nytimes.com/2010/08/22/magazine/22Adulthoodt. html?pagewanted=all&_r=0

Godin, Seth. "The map has been replaced by the compass". February 21, 2012. Web. 20 May. 2016 http://sethgodin. typepad.com/seths_blog/2012/02/the-map-has-been-replaced-by-the-compass.html

Goldstein, Meredith. "The quarter-life crises". The Boston Globe, 8 Sept 2004. Web. 20 May. 2016 http://archive.boston. com/yourlife/articles/2004/09/08/the_quarter_life_crisis/

Grossman, Lev. "Grow Up? Not So Fast". Time Magazine, 16 Jan 2005. Web. 20 May. 2016 http://content.time.com/time/ magazine/article/0,9171,1018089,00.html

Jobs, Steve. "You've Got to Find What You Love" Stanford News. June 2005. Web. 21 May. 2016 https://news.stanford. edu/2005/06/14/jobs-061505/

Komisar, Randy. "Goodbye Career, Hello Success." Harvard Business Review 1 Mar. 2000. Web. 20 May. 2016 https://hbr.org/2000/03/goodbye-careerhello-success

Lacy, Sarah. "Peter Thiel: We're in a Bubble and It's Not the Internet. It's Higher Education." Techcrunch 10 April 2011. Web. 20 May. 2016

http://techcrunch.com/2011/04/10/peter-thiel-were-in-a-bubble-and-its-not-the-internet-its-higher-education/

Newport, Cal. *So Good They Can't Ignore You: Why Skills Trump Passion in the Quest for Work You Love.* Business Plus, 2012. Print.

Perlin, Ross. *Intern Nation: How to Earn Nothing and Learn Little in the Brave New Economy.* Verso 2012. Print.

Riles, Eric. *The Lean Startup: How Constant Innovation Creates Radically Successful Businesses.* Penguin, 2011. Print.

Rumelt, Richard P. *Good Strategy Bad Strategy: The Difference.* Profile Books, 2011. Print.

Seligman, Martin E.P. *Flourish: A Visionary New Understanding of Happiness and Well-Being.* Nicholas Brealey Publishing, 2012. Print.

Seligman, Martin E.P. *Learned Optimism: How to Change Your Mind and Your Life.* Vintage Books, 2006. Print.

Singer, Peter. *The Most Good You Can Do: How Effective Altruism is Changing Ideas about Living Ethically.* Yale University, 2015. Print.

Swart, Tara, Chisholm, Kitty and Brown, Paul. *Neuroscience for Leadership: Harnessing the Brain Gain Advantage.* Palgrave MacMillan, 2012. Print.

Tyler, Eric. "Taking The Jeff Bezos Approach To Building Your Own Startup." Forbes 5 Dec. 2013. Web. 20 May. 2016 http://www.forbes.com/sites/realspin/2013/12/05/taking-the-jeff-bezos-approach-to-building-your-own-start-up/#ae896132e8a1

Tokumitsu, Miya. "In the Name of Love." Slate 16 Jan. 2014. Web. 20 May. 2016

http://www.slate.com/articles/technology/technology/2014/01/do_what_you_love_love_what_you_do_an_omnipresent_mantra_that_s_bad_for_work.html

Wilner, Abby and Robbins, Alexandra. *QuarterLife Crises, the Unique Challenges of Life in your Twenties*. Penguin Putnam, 2001. Print.

Young, Jeffrey E. and Klosko, Janet S. *Reinventing Your Life*. Plume, 1994. Print.

16670875R00078

Printed in Great Britain
by Amazon